ADE OKONRENDE

THE CALLED

Understanding the Spirituality of Calling

FOREWORD BY DR. JOSEPH OLEAR

THE CALLED

{Understanding the Spirituality of Calling}

PASTOR
ADE OKONRENDE

THE CALLED
{Understanding the Spirituality of Calling)
Author: Pastor Ade Okonrende
First Edition— November 2019

Contact: Pastor Ade Okonrende.
Email: okonrende@aol.com
Phone: 832 723 8470, 832 .372.0860

Inspiration: Holy Spirit

Chief Editor: Choice Okonrende

Cover design: Gfaydesigns
www.gfaydesigns.com 832.623.1201

Pagination and layout: Pastor Christy Ogbeide.
Christyogbeidebooks.com 832-661-4352

Books by the author are available at:
choiceworldpublishers.com
Amazon.com and leading bookshops

Printed in the United States of America

All scripture quotations are from the Amplified Bible
unless otherwise stated.

"THE CALLED"
[Understanding the Spirituality of Calling]

PREFACE

On a beautiful Monday afternoon, the 30th July 2019, my phone rang. It was a call from the Principal of the Bible College of the Redeemed Christian Church of God, Floyd, Texas USA, and Pastor [Dr.] Sayo Ajiboye. He requested that I do a teaching on the topic: "Understanding the Spirituality of Calling." Though my schedule was tight for any additional responsibility, however, I was prompted to accept his invitation and actually write a book on the topic. That was how the idea of writing "THE CALLED Understanding the Spirituality of Calling" was born.

The scripture says whatsoever is born of God overcomes the world. The first question that struck my mind was "What is the meaning of a call." Obviously there is a difference between a "Call" and a "Calling". It is important to recognize the identity of the "Caller". There will be the need to find out the state of "The Called" before and after the call took place. Was there any ground of preparation of "The Called"? The impact of a call will need be discussed. I was made to realize that the associates and associations of "The Called" would have tremendous effect on the fulfillment of the purpose of the call.

Everyone that is assigned to fulfill a purpose obviously will face some challenges. Understanding that success is not a game of accident but a deliberate effort that received divine endorsement. Everyone that is called would face challenges. "The called" may be a mono-talented or multi-talented individual. Records show that the multi-talented people face more challenges than people with basic gifting. Gifts and potentials are very crucial to the fulfillment of purpose but they are obviously not enough if not accompanied with character and appreciable charisma.

From scriptural analysis of some characters in the Bible, it is evident that the temperamental disposition of the individuals played vital role in their accomplishment of purpose. The role of the Holy Spirit in the life of an individual cannot be overemphasized. He is the greatest modifier of human disposition outside of environmental influence and pressure.

Pressure has been proven to be one of the greatest revealers of true value. Every one called into an assignment will surely come under pressure. There is no doubt that "Chocolate Soldiers" will melt at the instance of heat. Pressure reveals human qualities or animalistic traits. "The Called" may be confused by diverse pressures of life. Distorted information, prophesies or words of knowledge may put "The Called" under undue pressure. This is the place for a very good Spirit of discernment. A demand for implicit obedience puts man under great pressure. Many that were called by God fell victims of disobedience or the inability to discern the plan and purpose of God for their lives. A good example was Prophet Jonah; he was grossly diverted by the devil.

The "3Ds" Diversionary Devices of the Devil ("3Ds") have been the melting-pot of the experience of many that were called of the Lord. These diversions may be secular, matrimonial or ministerial. They are always beautifully packaged, attractive enough to lure or win the best of skeptics. They are baits of destruction. In most cases, they come as almost irresistible indulgences to the prospective victims. Very few survive the temptations of the baits.

It is very important for "The Called" to understand the spirituality of his or her calling. "The Called" must realize that he or she cannot fight spiritual battles with carnal weapons. Obviously, the methodology of Egypt will not thrive in Zion. If "The Called" would finish well, he or she must realize that "the flesh" is his or her greatest enemy.
Jesus said:
"It is the Spirit who gives life; the flesh conveys no benefit [it is of no account]. The words I have spoken to you are spirit and life [providing eternal life]."
John 6:63 AMP
"The Called" would remain an asset only if he or she finishes well; else the individual becomes a negative byword.

PROLOGUE

The narratives in this book are true life experience or observations. The plots are real, with little modification, for the purpose of clarity of expression. The characters are in some cases given stage-names, to conceal their true identities.

DEDICATION

This book is dedicated to the glory of God in appreciation of the role of my father and mentor in the Lord, Pastor E. A. Adeboye. He was used of the Lord to disciple me in my early days in the ministry, a service he has not ceased to render. I have learnt so much from him, such that I ask myself in some instances: "Would Daddy G.O. have done this? How would he have reacted in instances such as this? He remains himself and in his own class. I have my peculiarities and idiosyncrasies.

ACKNOWLEDGEMENT AND APPRECIATION

Thoughts could be very inspiring or frustrating. However there are some people who can turn your thoughts into exciting realities. I am blessed and highly favored by God to be surrounded by some of such gems of rare qualities.

I cannot but acknowledge Sister Ronke Popoola, Sis. Toyin Laditi, and Sis. Joke Alake who nurtured the tutelage of my literary prowess when I was in London [1990-1999]. I am happy to note that they have all made appreciable progress in the ministry.

I acknowledge my team of ministers and Christian workers who chose to give their time and skills for the final finish of this work:

Pastor (Dr.) Christy Ogbeide who did the pagination, Pastor Valentina Mozia and Deacon (Dr.) Olear who did the proofreading.

My dynamic Regional administrative secretary, Dcn. Olasumbo Babalola who worked with me to effect the corrections of the errors spotted by the proofreaders.
I am very grateful to Brother Chinedu Obeleagu, the church's administrative secretary who gave me enough ease to do my writings.

My profound appreciation and acknowledgement also goes to our son, Choice Okonrende the CEO of Choiceworld Publishers Inc. who in the pursuit of his Master's Degree program was not involved in the production of this book.

Great kudos to our only daughter, Deaconess Grace Aina; an indefatigable graphic Artist, Occupational therapist, Makeup Artist, Singer and Songwriter, Wife and Mother of three [GFay Designs] who designed the cover of this book.

My wife of inestimable value, [Pastor Grace Okonrende] is the main figure that made this book a possibility through her tolerance of my solitude and "boredom" while I did my writing in our bedroom. But for her, the vision would have been a mirage and "mission impossible".

May the Lord be with you all and send you reliable helpers of destiny.

FOREWORD

Pastor Ade Okonrende is currently the Regional Pastor in The Redeemed Christian Church of God, North America, Region 2, with ever increasing number of parishes. He has been a pastor for almost 40 years. His pastoral experience has enhanced his writing this book. He is a diligent, versatile and prolific author with numerous books to his credit. This book, "THE CALLED" however, is timely, unique and engaging. It is my prayer that readers will take heed of the admonitions in this book, to be good role models and mentors.

Pastor Ade's humble background clearly prepared him for writing "THE CALLED Understanding the spirituality of calling." Although from a poor background, his parents, especially his mother, guided him during his formative years. Pastor Ade did not allow his lowly beginning to discourage him, but the prayers of his mother and the blessings of his father surely have kept him on track. Abraham Lincoln's quote, "No man is poor, who has a godly mother," captures this foundational truth.

"THE. CALLED" gives a beacon of hope and a source of inspiration to Christians globally.

Prophet Isaiah had "unclean lips", yet God used him. (Isaiah 6:5.) Apostle Paul tortured Christians before his Damascus experience [Acts 7 and 9], yet God used him immensely. The Scripture says in 1 Corinthians 15:10 "But by the grace (the unmerited favor and blessing) of God I am what I am, and His grace toward me was not [found to be] for nothing (fruitless and without effect). In fact, I worked harder than all of them [the apostles], though it was not really I but the grace (the unmerited favor and blessing) of God which was with me."

Pastor Ade Okonrende has labored in his calling and this no doubt, is due to the special grace of God.

"THE CALLED" is about the story of a man who wriggled out of the cocoon of poverty, was not crushed by peer pressure, survived the prejudice of man and was not deterred by the disdain of so-called experts. God raised "Cardo" [Donald] — the hero of this book, from his lowly beginning to the dizzying heights of success.

The author admonishes readers that: "Vessels chosen by God are always the devil's targets; he does not make cheap choices." Some Christian workers in their naivety, trivialize the spirituality of their callings. Unfortunately, the devil targets the "Spiritual Giants" whose fall, he believes, will discourage or derail others.

But, how do we avoid this fall? How do we sustain the momentum in this Christian race? The answers will be found in this book.

"THE CALLED" written in an almost conversational and engaging style, is compelling as well as entertaining. I strongly recommend it.

Adhering to the counsel in this book, having a good mentor and walking closely with God will shape the reader's vision and help him or her to navigate the Christian journey.
May God uphold us all to the end. Amen

Dr Joseph Olear

TABLE OF CONTENTS

CHAPTER ONE

THE CALL THAT PRECEDES THE CALLING

It was a very frustrating moment in the life of "Cardo" as he was nicknamed in his high school days. He was very rascally. He was a transfer student from Gasikya College, Cardozo Village. His rascality earned him the abbreviation of the school he hailed from. He maintained his rascality till his first year in college. He viewed his notoriety as popularity. Due to distractions and reveling, he was unable to score a pass mark in some of his class tests. He was dating a classmate of his, who actually scored higher marks. than he did in same test. His fear of failure and prospective disgrace at the end of the academic session prompted him to be a little more serious with his studies. He was determined to study in the evening of the faithful day 23rd of May 1977. There was a power-outage. In his impetuous anger, he realized that his roommate had invited him to a Christian drama that was slated for the same day. He had the impression that his reading lantern must have been taken to the said Christian meeting without his permission. He was determined to track down Peter, his roommate. He headed for the venue of the Christian meeting.

He was very hostile to everyone that crossed his way, kicked every empty can and paper-balls off his path as he aggressively headed for the auditorium to apprehend his roommate for his missing lantern. In his thoughts, he adjudged Peter as a complete modest Christian who would not fight back if he slapped him on the face. He knew the implications of such aggressions or assault if it happened on the university campus. He was confident that he would easily get away with it. He laughed as he soliloquized; "...All he would do is to pray for me that his Father God should forgive me for I knew not what I did." He was lost in thought as he walked down the staggered sloppy terrace of the dark auditorium. The drama was already in session and the lights switched off but for the stage-lights. He made frantic efforts, screening the crowd in the dark. One of the seated observers touched him and showed him an empty seat. It was like a divinely orchestrated touch as he sat down almost mesmerized and compelled to watch the ongoing drama. He was given a brief narrative of how far the drama had gone. The title of the play was: "THE LONG-SEARCH," written and acted by a Christian group from a university few hundred miles away.

He was captivated by the scenes. He felt the play was a complete replay of his personal life. He recalled his childhood days, in the promiscuous environment where he grew up. He could not imagine how terrible it was that he grew up blowing disposed condoms as toy balloons. In his ruminations, he conclusively agreed that he would ruin his life if he continued in the order of his promiscuity and licentiousness. He finally decided to give his life to Jesus Christ. Not like in his pretentious past. He had been invited to various Christian meetings at which he answered the altar call, just to please or placate those who invited him to the meeting. He had never at any point in time actually surrendered his life to Christ in its fullness.

At the end of the drama, an altar call was made. He was actually waiting for the call. He probably was the very first person to put his hand up in response to the altar call. He anticipated the usual invitation to come to the front. He was not disappointed. He went straight to the front of the stage. The converts were celebrated by the clap of hands and were divided into various groups for counseling. Cardo was in a group of five and was to be counseled by a young lady. He was captivated by the beauty of the young lady and her sonorous voice. To him, the voice was thrilling than the content of her counseling. As the lady was rounding off her very impressive counseling session, she asked: "Does anyone have a question?" Cardo indicated that he had one or two questions. He was just lustful and desirous to hear the voice of the lady for a longer time. His question was: "How would someone know when he or she actually becomes a true child of God." The counselor responded: "I cannot tell you all that it takes or when a person actually becomes a child of God just at a sitting like tonight." However she flipped her very small handy Bible open and read:

"Now the practices of the sinful nature are clearly evident: they are sexual immorality, impurity, sensuality (total irresponsibility, lack of self-control), idolatry, sorcery, hostility, strife, jealousy, fits of anger, disputes, dissensions, factions [that promote heresies], envy, drunkenness, riotous behavior, and other things like these. I warn you beforehand, just as I did previously, that those who practice such things will not inherit the kingdom of God. But the fruit of the Spirit [the result of His presence within us] is love [unselfish concern for others], joy, [inner] peace, patience [not the ability to wait, but how we act while waiting], kindness, goodness, faithfulness, gentleness, self-control. Against such things there is no law. And those who belong to Christ Jesus have crucified the sinful nature together with its passions and appetites. If we [claim to] live by the [Holy] Spirit, we must also walk by the Spirit [with personal integrity, godly character, and moral courage—our conduct empowered by the Holy Spirit]. We must not become conceited, challenging or provoking one another, envying one another." Galatians 5:19-26 AMP

Though convicted of sin, Cardo wanted to hear the lady speak a little further. He asked: "Am I now a child of God?" The lady hesitated and was very courteous in her answer. She opened her Bible and read from the gospel of John 1: 10-13.

"He (Christ) was in the world, and though the world was made through Him, the world did not recognize Him. He came to that which was His own [that which belonged to Him—His world, His creation, His possession], and those who were His own [people— the Jewish nation] did not receive and welcome Him. But to as many as did receive and welcome Him, He gave the right [the authority, the privilege] to become children of God, that is, to those who believe in (adhere to, trust in, and rely on) His name— who were born, not of blood [natural conception], nor of the will of the flesh [physical impulse], nor of the will of man [that of a natural father], but of God [that is, a divine and supernatural birth—they are born of God— spiritually transformed, renewed, sanctified]."

She conclusively said: "Now you have the right to become a child of God if you take your decision to follow Jesus with all seriousness as reflected in Apostle Paul's letter to us all, as stated in Phil. 2: 12:

"So then, my dear ones, just as you have always obeyed [my instructions with enthusiasm], not only in my presence, but now much more in my absence, continue to work out your salvation [that is, cultivate it, bring it to full effect, actively pursue spiritual maturity] with awe-inspired fear and trembling [using serious caution and critical self-evaluation to avoid anything that might offend God or discredit the name of Christ]."

It was time to pray, bringing the counseling session to a close. The counselor asked the converts to return the decision slips. Cardo had not filled his own due to his vain imagination about the beauty of the young counselor. Though his mindset had changed, he remained in the rumination on the beauty of his counselor. In his thought, he concluded: "If a beautiful lady of this immensity can be found amongst the "Born-again" what else would I be looking for out there in the world of sinners?" He filled out the form with all sincerity. In his rascality, he would have given wrong information so that it will be impossible for the brethren to track him down on campus. He was the last to hand in his decision slip. The lady counselor had gone to attend to other issues. The officer who collected the slip from him happened to be a friend of his "wanted" roommate. He called Bro. Peter to come and see the evidence of answered prayers. Bro. Peter could hardly believe his eyes. He jumped on the neck of his previous emotional tormentor and unidentified potential assailant. Cardo was surprised about the response of almost all the brethren that were around.

Little did he know that the salvation of his soul had been the regular prayer request of his roommate. All the brethren received him into the fold with great joy and amazement. In his imagination, he could not believe why they were all so highly excited about his decision to give his life to Jesus. The joy and rejoicing of the brethren called the attention of virtually everyone around. The beautiful counselor turned to watch what was going on. She saw Cardo and was more curious to know more about what she thought must be a big catch. Her response was very exciting to Cardo. She gave him a congratulatory handshake. He was well pleased that she gave him a handshake. Her soft palm sent a message to his old carnal nature. He quickly shut off the vain imagination as he ruminated on Galatians 5: 19 which were previously read to him during the counseling session. He counseled himself and informed his "flesh" I am now a child of God." His understanding of John 1: 12 was that his response to the altar call made him a child of God. He was not a cheap catch but a big catch for the Lord. His decision to follow Jesus attested to the saying that "The devil does not make a cheap choice". Neither did God. No child of God should consider himself or herself cheap.

Every soul saved is a precious asset in God's plan to pull the devil's kingdom down. God is the maker; He makes the individual a threshing instrument subject to his or her yield to the dictates of the Holy Spirit. Isaiah 41: 15 reads:

"In fact, I have made of you a new, sharp threshing implement with sharp edges; You will thresh the mountains and crush them, and make the hills like chaff." Isaiah 41:15 AMP

He was full of the joy of salvation as he walked out of the auditorium. He was surprised to realize that some of his friends were waiting for him just at the entrance of the auditorium. He walked into them in complete innocence. He was pulled back by one of them and charged a decedent for his attempt to leave the group. "We saw you go out to join the "SU"! [The term "SU" was in those days used derogatorily to describe a Christian sect that were viewed as extremists and fanatical about Christianity. The Scripture Union was then the foremost evangelistic group in the country.] Cardo, though ignorant of the impact of the Holy Spirit upon his soul was very bold in his response, "Tonight is a different night, I did not respond to join the "SUs" but I have actually given my life to Jesus. There is no pretense tonight at all." With a tincture of smile, looking into the eyes of one of his very close Allies he said: "You'll remember we both went out to please them at some of those meetings."

With a broad laughter his friend responded: "The game continues..." Cardo was very impatient to tolerate any idea that suggested he was not a 'true child of God.' He was very unequivocal when he said: "Sorry, I am out of all these," I am not into any game; I have decided to follow Jesus and there is no turning back." There was a row of laughter. He was surprised at what prompted the laughter which he viewed as an acrimony. One of them sarcastically said: "He loved that beautiful lady that was mandated to talk to him when he went out. I am sure that was the driving force." He felt indicted; the indictment brought back his conviction of the sin of lustful imaginations but triggered a righteous indignation in him. He determined to prove his old friends wrong. With a frown on his face and a quiver in his voice, he said: "If you see me anymore as a member of this sinful, worldly group, you are making a big mistake. If I ever do those bad stuffs, call me a bastard." He was walking away when they chorused: "Son of God, the heavenly man, no more of this world." "So I am" he responded.

Of all the brethren, Peter was the happiest. He was very anxious to meet his roommate at their hall of residence. He was a little agitated because on his way out of the auditorium, he saw him engaged in conversation with his group of friends. He was scared that they might have tried to convince him not to keep his declaration for Jesus. To him, it was a battle for the soul. He determined to do his best to see him completely sold out to the Lord. He himself was well disciplined and determined to do the same to other souls. The night was the beginning of a wonderful relationship between Cardo and Peter, his one-time estranged roommate. He recalled how he used to lock Peter out when he had illicit sexual relationships with his girlfriend Doris. He could not get over the tolerance and endurance of Peter. He determined to, at least become a Christian like him. They prayed together for the very first time. Peter had in the past spoken to him about Jesus and asked him if he could pray with him; the proposals were declined with flimsy excuses. The love of Christ became their great unifier.

Cardo was anxious to know more about Jesus Christ. He felt he needed to build a good defense for his new found faith so that he would be able to successfully respond to the anticipated inquisitions of his friends, members of his immediate and extended family. He would not miss any of the fellowships. The brethren showered so much love of Christ on him, to fully convince him that life is better with Christ than in the world of sin. He was given some special treat by the brethren. He felt there was nothing good outside of Christ. He determined to break up the relationship between him and his well-known girlfriend on campus and the unknown ones. In one of his soliloquies, he said: "The devil is wicked. How was I comfortable dating someone else's wife. How was I ready to procure abortion for which I was not responsible? With a stretched deep breath, he said: "I thank God that I survived the infections of various sexually transmitted diseases. Oh no, there is nothing good to return to in the world of sin," he conclusively asserted. He determined never to have illicit sex but was deeply engrossed with masturbation.

Peter saw Cardo as his personal spiritual baby and was ready to fully disciple him. He taught him so many Christian principles to enhance his spiritual growth. No one knew about his secret practice of masturbation. He felt very guilty every time he practiced it. He could not confess or own up to anyone that he practiced the secret sin of spiritual, moral and emotional impurity. His agitations compelled his asking multiple questions both at fellowship meetings and during discussions with his mentors; Bro. Peter. Some of the questions he asked his mentor were: "When does a person fully become a child of God? Can a Christian be completely free from committing sin?" Peter knew the sensitivity of the questions and the frailty of a new born-babe in Christ. He was not going to sound offensive, neither was he ready to compromise the truth of the word of God. "I am very happy for your inquisitions. They are evident of a burning desire to be a true child of God." The phrase: 'True child of God' caught his attention. His gaze at Peter said a lot about his desire to know more.

The semester was almost over. Peter felt the need to do a good job on the discipleship of Cardo before the holidays roll in. He anticipated he may face some challenges during the holidays. One of the evenings, he turned to Cardo and said: "I thank God for His grace upon my life and who I am today in Him. It had not been an easy road. I am happy for you. I did not get it straight and direct when I gave my life to Jesus but I eventually got in touch with a wonderful pastor who took up the responsibility of mentoring me. You have actually started well and I believe and desire that you are actually doing well. Before I gave my life to Christ, I was very sexually loose. I took some very bad lines of action." The countenance of Cardo brightened up as he could identify with the experience of his mentor. "Though I did not go after any lady but I was grossly involved in masturbation. I felt I was not doing evil against anybody. My assumption was proved wrong when my pastor preached that those who masturbate may actually not cause damages to others but to themselves. He said such individuals sell themselves to invisible demonic spiritual spouses that may ruin their fortune or prospect in life. He was of the opinion that masturbation is partly responsible for diverse life challenges and matrimonial disorder."

The statements hit him hard but he was ashamed to tell Peter that he was already a victim of masturbation. He determined to stop the act of self-destruction. He was very impressed that his mentor was not ashamed to share his personal past challenges and failures. In his heart, he determined to always open up to Peter on the challenges of his life.

"There is a great joy in becoming a child of God. One of the Bible passages that were expounded to my understanding when I gave my life to Jesus was: "Little children (believers, dear ones), do not let anyone lead you astray. The one who practices righteousness [the one who strives to live a consistently honorable life—in private as well as in public—and to conform to God's precepts] is righteous, just as He is righteous. The one who practices sin [separating himself from God, and offending Him by acts of disobedience, indifference, or rebellion] is of the devil [and takes his inner character and moral values from him, not God]; for the devil has sinned and violated God's law from the beginning. The Son of God appeared for this purpose, to destroy the works of the devil. No one who is born of God [deliberately, knowingly, and habitually] practices sin, because God's seed [His principle of life, the essence of His righteous character] remains [permanently] in him [who is born again—who is reborn from above—spiritually transformed, renewed, and set apart for His purpose]; and he [who is born again] cannot habitually [live a life characterized by] sin, because he is born of God and longs to please Him."1 John 3:7-9 AMP

Peter observed that the countenance of his mentee dropped. He laid his left hand on his shoulder as a mark of encouragement, and said: "You have the power, authority and enablement to live above sin. That was the power given to you the very moment you decided to give your life to Jesus. He took his Bible and read: "But to as many as did receive and welcome Him, He gave the right [the authority, the privilege] to become children of God, that is, to those who believe in (adhere to, trust in, and rely on) His name" John1:12 AMP

The version of Cardo's Bible read: "Power to become" Cardo, a little agitated, questioned: "Are we not supposed to be reading the same Bible?" Peter had to explain that there are diverse versions of the Holy Bible. He reiterated that the same word was interpreted as power, right, and authority. He was, however, of the opinion that the word 'right' was very misleading. He claimed that power and authority are more compelling on the mind of any determined convert who desires to grow. With a broad smile, he said: "Let us agree that you have been given the power to become a child of God. Please realize that power may be dormant and useless if not exercised." Cardo nodded his head in approval. "It means that without the exercise of 'the power to become', one may not actually "become"; I mean, grow to behave and act as expected of a child of God." "This is deep. So, I have to determine to become a child of God?" "Yes, Peter asserted.

Peter felt it was the appropriate time for him to push some hard truth down the throat of his convert. He said: "Let us read some of these Bible passages and you will see that the Bible is clear on potential good Christian doing his or her part to become a true child of God." He opened to Galatians 4: 19, reading through the text:

"My little children, for whom I am again in [the pains of] labor until Christ is [completely and permanently] formed within you."

Cardo was apt to ask: "Can one answer the altar call and remain in fellowship without Christ being formed in the person?" "That is what apostle Paul was talking about. There is no doubt that many of the converts in churches today may not have Christ formed in them. The fact is that growth determines maturity and acquisition of the nature of Christ through His Spirit." He took his Bible, opened and read:

"However, you are not [living] in the flesh [controlled by the sinful nature] but in the Spirit, if in fact the Spirit of God lives in you [directing and guiding you]. But if anyone does not have the Spirit of Christ, he does not belong to Him [and is not a child of God]." Romans 8:9 AMP

He laid emphasis on the closing part of the verse, "But if anyone does not have the Spirit of Christ, he does not belong to Him [and is not a child of God]." "Is it possible to be converted without having the Spirit of Christ?" Cardo questioned. "The fact is that it is possible to answer altar call and remain in fellowship with other brethren without receiving the spirit of Christ and become a child of God. The fact is that the Holy Spirit convicted the individual of sin but does not imply that Christ had been formed in the individual. The Spirit of Christ comes into a convert when the conviction to follow Jesus is well nurtured through compliance with the word of God and prayers out of a pure heart. The incomplete circle of these lines of action is responsible for the challenges we find in 'Christendom' today." Peter suggested they should go to bed and reserve other questions for the near future. He however gave Cardo the mandate to read: Romans. 1: 7. Phil. 2: 12-13 Colossians. 2: 6-8

Cardo very strongly desired to make the best of his decision to follow Jesus Christ, especially because of the pressure of his friends and their compelling desire to have him back in their group. He was constantly reminded by the Holy Spirit that he has laid his hands on the plough and must not look back. His friends had schooled his former girlfriend not to give up in her hope to have him return. She was to lure him into just one moment of sexual relationship.

In his hunger for the word, he decided to read the texts before he went to bed.

"[I am writing] to all who are beloved of God in Rome, called to be saints (God's people) and set apart for a sanctified life, [that is, set apart for God and His purpose]: Grace to you and peace [inner calm and spiritual well-being] from God our Father and from the Lord Jesus Christ." Romans 1:7 AMP

"So then, my dear ones, just as you have always obeyed [my instructions with enthusiasm], not only in my presence, but now much more in my absence, continue to work out your salvation [that is, cultivate it, bring it to full effect, actively pursue spiritual maturity] with awe-inspired fear and trembling [using serious caution and critical self-evaluation to avoid anything that might offend God or discredit the name of Christ]. For it is [not your strength, but it is] God who is effectively at work in you, both to will and to work [that is, strengthening, energizing, and creating in you the longing and the ability to fulfill your purpose] for His good pleasure." Phil. 2:12-13 AMP

"Therefore as you have received Christ Jesus the Lord, walk in [union with] Him [reflecting His character in the things you do and say—living lives that lead others away from sin], having been deeply rooted [in Him] and now being continually built up in Him and [becoming increasingly more] established in your faith, just as you were taught, and overflowing in it with gratitude. See to it that no one takes you captive through philosophy and empty deception [pseudo-intellectual babble], according to the tradition [and musings] of mere men, following the elementary principles of this world, rather than following [the truth... the teachings of] Christ." Colossians 2:6-8 AMP

In the morning, he suddenly had the burning desire to go and witness to his "old flame" before they all parted at the end of the semester. He headed for her room and was very well received. He was bombarded with many questions on his new-found faith in Christ. Debby was affirmative that she was also a Christian. With a smile, he said to her: "Just like I was while we were together." She looked at him lustfully. His body reacted as he looked through her translucent night gown. He felt very uncomfortable. Debby moved closer to him. He sensed a moment of danger as he felt very turgid. He rose up from his sitting position and rested on the book shelf to hide away his almost conspicuous undesired but uncontrollable turgidity. Debby rose up to embrace him. At that moment, he was speedily reminded that he cannot afford to drag Jesus in the mud. He bolted away from the room and ran straight to his hall of residence. He was panting as he ran into the room. He went on his knees as he continued to chant: "Thank you, Jesus." He knew it was a close shave with sin. He did not feel condemned because in his heart he did not go there for that purpose. He had a better understanding of the verse of the Bible that says: "Flee from every appearance of evil". He shouted: "Praise the Lord. Now I know that I am a new creature in Christ Jesus."

He laughed very wildly and shouted: "Satan you are a loser. I am saved in Christ Jesus. I have answered His call and there is no going back." The door opened behind him and it was Peter his roommate and mentor. "Was any battle going on? While I was approaching the door, I heard you shouting at the devil." "O yes, I had to. It was a shout of victory." He narrated his experience. He was cautioned that it was dangerous to go alone on such a mission. "That was a lesson." He responded. "Would you want me to go with you when next you choose to visit her?" Peter asked. "NO" He responded, sharply. I may give you and the evangelistic team her details in efforts to save her soul. As for me, I will stay away. I pray I will be preserved blameless unto the coming of Jesus." With a smile, Peter opened and read:

"Now may the God of peace Himself sanctify you through and through [that is, separate you from profane and vulgar things, make you pure and whole and undamaged—consecrated to Him—set apart for His purpose]; and may your spirit and soul and body be kept complete and [be found] blameless at the coming of our Lord Jesus Christ. Faithful and

absolutely trustworthy is He who is calling you [to Himself for your salvation], and He will do it [He will fulfill His call by making you holy, guarding you, watching over you, and protecting you as His own]."
1 Thessalonians 5:23-24 AMP

The semester exams were over and Peter was set to change school. He knew he may not come in contact with his spiritual baby for a long time or ever. Just the night before they parted, he said to Cardo; "Bro. I want to thank God for the opportunity that He gave me to be your roommate. It started as a torture but now a pleasure. We are about to part, assumedly for a while. I am not too happy to inform you that I will not be returning to this campus in the next academic session. I have been offered admission to study engineering in another institution." Cardo was very sad because of the news, but was happy for him to pursue his desired line of studies.

Peter, with tears almost rolling down his cheeks said: "It is my prayer that you survive the challenges of early spiritual childhood. I have tried to lay the foundation for you to build on. Just as Apostle Paul wrote:

"According to the [remarkable] grace of God which was given to me [to prepare me for my task], like a skillful master builder I laid a foundation, and now another is building on it. But each one must be careful how he builds on it, for no one can lay a foundation other than the one which is [already] laid, which is Jesus Christ. But if anyone builds on the foundation with gold, silver, precious stones, wood, hay, straw, each one's work will be clearly shown [for what it is]; for the day [of judgment] will disclose it, because it is to be revealed with fire, and the fire will test the quality and character and worth of each person's work. If any person's work which he has built [on this foundation, that is, any outcome of his effort] remains [and survives this test], he will receive a reward. But if any person's work is burned up [by the test], he will suffer the loss [of his reward]; yet he himself will be saved, but only as [one who has barely escaped] through fire."1 Corinthians 3:10-15 AMP

It was Cardo's first time of reading the text. He was surprised that the work of a Christian could be burnt. There were diverse thoughts and questions running through his mind. He was about to request for permission to ask some questions when Peter said: "Please feel free to ask any question; do not feel you may be intruding into my privacy. Since I gave my life to Jesus, I have become a public figure, ready for scrutiny at any point in time." His assertion of self-confidence was very intriguing. Cardo was very inquisitive, and asked: "Now that you got me to stop the practice of masturbation..." Peter interrupted him by saying: 'You meant you were convicted by the Holy Spirit to stop masturbating. I do not have the power to stop you. If He spoke to your heart to stop the evil and self-destructive practice, He must have shown you great love and enablement," he asserted. Cardo was melancholic as he said: "I had a big struggle before I overcame it. I had been involved in the practice before I became born-again. It was the devil's suggested preferred evil for my sexual promiscuity." "Congratulations on your victory, believing you will never again fall a victim." He opened his Bible and read:

"For if I [or anyone else should] rebuild [through word or by practice] what I once tore down [the belief that observing the Law is essential for salvation], I prove myself to be a transgressor."Galatians 2:18 AMP

Before we part, please let me bring up some of the questions I was going to ask. "How do you control your passion for sex"? "Love the Lord," he responded. "How?" "Peter came up with a counter question, "What did you tell the ladies before you slept with them?" "I love you." They both laughed realizing that they have bastardized the meaning of love. Peter went on: "You knew that, that was not a true love. You will now have to ask the Holy Spirit to guide you through as you make an analytical study of Apostle Paul's letter to us all:

"If I give all my possessions to feed the poor, and if I surrender my body to be burned, but do not have love, it does me no good at all. Love endures with patience and serenity, love is kind and thoughtful, and is not jealous or envious; love does not brag and is not proud or arrogant. It is not rude; it is not self-seeking, it is not provoked [nor overly sensitive and easily angered]; it does not take into account a wrong endured. It does not rejoice at injustice, but rejoices with the truth [when right and truth prevail]. Love bears all things [regardless of what comes], believes all things [looking for the best in each one], hopes all things [remaining steadfast during difficult times], and endures all things [without weakening]. Love never fails [it never fades nor ends]. But as for prophecies, they will pass away; as for tongues, they will cease; as for the gift of special knowledge, it will pass away. For we know in part, and we prophesy in part [for our knowledge is fragmentary and incomplete]. But when that which is complete and perfect comes, that which is incomplete and partial will pass away."

1 Corinthians 13:3-10 AMP

After they read the scripture, Peter said; "If you have a good understanding of what we just read, your love for God will make you give yourself to Him as a living sacrifice. He read from Romans 12: 1-2

"Therefore I urge you, brothers and sisters, by the mercies of God, to present your bodies [dedicating all of yourselves, set apart] as a living sacrifice, holy and well-pleasing to God, which is your rational (logical, intelligent) act of worship. And do not be conformed to this world [any longer with its superficial values and customs], but be transformed and progressively changed [as you mature spiritually] by the renewing of your mind [focusing on godly values and ethical attitudes], so that you may prove [for yourselves] what the will of God is, that which is good and acceptable and perfect [in His plan and purpose for you]."

With a tincture of seriousness, he reiterated: "A living sacrifice has choices but yields himself or herself to the dictates of the Lord. The Bible will come alive in your heart as you keep yourself occupied with the Great Commission. Your busy schedules will limit your exposures to temptations. You also have to determine to mortify your members as Apostle Paul wrote to us in his letter to the Colossians.": "So put to death and deprive of power the evil longings of your earthly body [with its sensual, self-centered instincts] immorality, impurity, sinful passion, evil desire, and greed, which is [a kind of] idolatry [because it replaces your devotion to God]. Because of these [sinful] things the [divine] wrath of God is coming on the sons of disobedience [those who fail to listen and who routinely and obstinately disregard God's precepts], and in these [sinful things] you also once walked, when you were habitually living in them [without the knowledge of Christ]. But now rid yourselves [completely] of all these things: anger, rage, malice, slander, and obscene (abusive, filthy, vulgar) language from your mouth. Do not lie to one another, for you have stripped off the old self with its evil practices, and have put on the new [spiritual] self who is being continually renewed in true knowledge in the image of Him who created the new self" Colossians 3:5-10 AMP

Then you can comfortably quote:
"Therefore I do not run without a definite goal; I do not flail around like one beating the air [just shadow boxing]. But [like a boxer] I strictly discipline my body and make it my slave, so that, after I have preached [the gospel] to others, I myself will not somehow be disqualified [as unfit for service]."
1 Corinthians 9:26-27 AMP

By the time you have complied with the dictates of these texts, you can confidently declare:
"I have been crucified with Christ [that is, in Him I have shared His crucifixion]; it is no longer I who live, but Christ lives in me. The life I now live in the body I live by faith [by adhering to, relying on, and completely trusting] in the Son of God, who loved me and gave Himself up for me."Galatians 2:20 AMP.

It will be possible for you to say:
"I know how to get along and live humbly [in difficult times], and I also know how to enjoy abundance and live in prosperity. In any and every circumstance I have learned the secret [of facing life], whether well-

fed or going hungry, whether having an abundance or being in need. I can do all things [which He has called me to do] through Him who strengthens and empowers me [to fulfill His purpose—I am self-sufficient in Christ's sufficiency; I am ready for anything and equal to anything through Him who infuses me with inner strength and confident peace.]" Philippians 4:12-13 AMP

"I guess I must have answered most of the questions you may wish to ask," he concluded. "Yes Sir, you actually did. Remember you once told me that he who loves protects the interest of the loved. I promise you that by the grace of God, I will surely live to protect the interest of the Lord. I will not crucify him afresh or put him to open shame. I believe I have already fully answered His call." The parting was very emotional. They hugged each other as they wept. Peter in his valedictory statement said: "Though we are parting now, surely if we both keep our promises and profession of faith, we shall surely meet again at the marriage supper of the Lamb. If I were to determine what happens, I would love that we remain together for our three year program but I am fully persuaded that the scripture says:

"And we know [with great confidence] that God [who is deeply concerned about us] causes all things to work together [as a plan] for good for those who love

God, to those who are called according to His plan and purpose." Romans 8:28 AMP

"My final statement to us both was written by Apostle Peter, stated in 2 Peter 1: 10-11."

"*Therefore, believers, be all the more diligent to make certain about His calling and choosing you [be sure that your behavior reflects and confirms your relationship with God]; for by doing these things [actively developing these virtues], you will never stumble [in your spiritual growth and will live a life that leads others away from sin]; for in this way entry into the eternal kingdom of our Lord and Savior Jesus Christ will be abundantly provided to you.*"

"You have successfully answered the call of the master. May you recognize 'your calling' when the time comes."

A living sacrifice has choices but yields
himself or herself to the dictates of the Lord.

CHAPTER TWO

THE CALLING

A response, submission and surrender to a call instigate a calling. It is a common saying that; "Many are called but few are chosen." The chosen are the ones that have a calling. There is no choice without a purpose, function and desired accomplishment by the one who made the choice. A call could be very encompassing. Making a choice is being specific with a mandate. Calling is therefore a call to and for a specific function in efforts to achieve a desired accomplishment. A chosen vessel is a tool in the hands of the one who made him or her a choice. A tool is subject to the initiatives and dictates of the one who chose it for a given task. God would never put blame on His tools. He has the right and authority to place, replace or displace any of His "tools". God prepares His vessel or tool ahead of the appointed time of use. In most cases, human experiences, trials, challenges, predicaments or moments of comfort are preparatory to the divine assignment. The Preacher [King Solomon] wrote:

"If the axe is dull and he does not sharpen its edge, then he must exert more strength; but wisdom [to sharpen the axe] helps him succeed [with less effort]."
Ecclesiastes 10:10 AMP

The accomplishment of a chosen tool is subject to the ability and prowess of the one that made the choice.

When Jesus chose His disciples, He said to them "...I will make you fishers of men" He was not looking out for their individual ability but availability. He makes "the tool" to become what it could. He had a variety of choices and equally qualified prospective candidates. Every appointed disciple given a calling was a beneficiary of divine opportunity. He developed their potentials based on their readiness to make the best of opportunities and privileges. The attainments of each of the disciples were not determined by the presence of the Lord but by their personal character traits and submission to the dictates of the Lord. Their responses and attitudes to the call, spelt out their respective calling.

Andrew was noted for his ability to reach out to others.

Peter was credited for his in-depth human analysis and adventure.

Matthew was noted for his corporate and organizational ability.

James and John, the sons of Zebedee, were recognized for their ego and ambition.

John, the beloved was a tenacious, reserved and reliable disciple.

Judas Iscariot was an identified thief.

Being in the ministry may not be of significant impact if the individual is not in absolute surrender to the Holy Spirit.

The recognition of the identity of the caller is very crucial to the calling of any individual in the ministry. When the caller is not identified or recognized, "The Called" may operate in confusion and contentions. He or she may contend with those who have adequate knowledge of the Lord Jesus as the one who called them unto ministry. When Apostle Paul (Saul of Tarsus) was called unto salvation, he questioned the identity of his caller. On recognition of the Savior of his soul, he asked for the purpose of his calling. The scripture states:

"As he traveled he approached Damascus, and suddenly a light from heaven flashed around him [displaying the glory and majesty of Christ]; and he fell to the ground and heard a voice [from heaven] saying to him, "Saul, Saul, why are you persecuting and oppressing Me?" And Saul said, "Who are You, Lord?" And He answered, "I am Jesus whom you are persecuting, now get up and go into the city, and you will be told what you must do." Acts 9:3-6 AMP

Until "the called" realizes the purpose and spirituality of his or her calling, abuse, misuse or failure may become inevitable.

Moses was prepared and called of God to liberate the children of Israel. Exodus 3:1-12

Nehemiah was called for the purpose of rebuilding of the walls of Jerusalem. Nehemiah 2: 1-end

Samuel was called by God to become a judge in Israel. 1Sam. 3: 1-end

David was called and chosen to deliver and lead the children of Israel. 1Samuel. 16; 1-13

Apostle Peter was repeatedly called by the Lord Jesus to lead the apostles of old. Luke 5: 1-11, John 21: 1-19.

Apostle Paul was called to take the gospel to the Gentiles. Acts 9: 1-30, Romans. 11: 12-14.

It was their obedience to the initial call unto salvation that afforded them the privilege of having a calling in the ministry.

Cardo was curious to know the area of his calling in the ministry. He was always anxious to attend Christian meetings. He had the least idea of what a standard Christian ministry is all about. He would listen to any preacher. He heard some statements that he strongly disagreed with. The preacher said: "I want to assure you that if you give your life to Jesus today, you become a child of God. Your Father, God will from today has the responsibility of protecting you. You are saved and safe with Jesus and heaven awaits you." He saw the statement as very enticing but a partial contradiction of what he was taught by his mentor when he answered the call unto salvation. In such instances, he probed through his Bible to authenticate the claim of the preacher. He had a personal determination to be a "Berean Christian." He had fallen in love with the statement of Doctor Luke written in the book of Acts of the Apostles:

"The brothers immediately sent Paul and Silas away by night to Berea; and when they arrived, they entered

the Jewish synagogue. Now these people were more noble and open-minded than those in Thessalonica, so they received the message [of salvation through faith in the Christ] with great eagerness, examining the Scriptures daily to see if these things were so."
Acts 17:10-11AMP

In most cases, he was not able to come to a conclusive truth until he shared the conflicting information with some of his trusted members in the fellowship. He had a personal conviction that spiritual nobility comes through the submission to the Holy Spirit and adequate knowledge of the scriptures.

As the holidays set in, he decided to return to the church he attended in pretense for years before he eventually became born-again on campus. He realized that what kept him in the church in his days of deceit was not his love for the Lord but his ardent love for soccer. He was invited by his friends to help them in one of the championships. Since then he kept the company of many of his teammates who attended the church. He knew he was not born-again but would not want to miss the company of his teammates, especially because they had many things in common. He determined to do his best to effect some changes in the lifestyles of his old friends. He believed that was his first assignment. He remembered he had tried same on the last of his chain of girls. He was of the opinion that talking to and trying to influence his old friends may not be as dangerous an experience.

Ruminating over his past and how he perfectly blended with the brethren in the church, prior to the genuine salvation of his soul, he believed it was an error to have always addressed him as a Christian brother. He saw the church as a place of piety and righteousness, so he chose not to be addressed as "Cardo" but Bro. Donald. He believed prior to his genuine salvation, he could have successfully dated, defiled or married any of the sincere Christian sisters. His personal experience taught him about the danger of assumptions and presumptions. He was always sensitive to the lifestyles of all of his brethren. He paid attention to their actions and reactions to issues. He screened their contributions during discussions so as to identify their value placements. He believed that an individual's value placement shapes the character.

He listened to his pastor, Gabriel O'Far preach a sermon on the topic: "Men of Honest Report." The text was taken from Acts 6: 1-6. With emphasis on the third verse:

"Therefore, brothers, choose from among you seven men with good reputations [men of godly character and moral integrity], full of the Spirit and of wisdom, whom we may put in charge of this task."Acts 6:3 AMP

His own version of the Bible read: "... Men of good report." While the pastor's version read: "Men of honest report," it was the King James Version. This reiterated what his first mentor had told him that same Hebrew or Greek words could be interpreted using diverse words in English or other languages but imply the same meaning or convey the same message. He concluded that honesty is synonymous with good. He chose to be honest in all his dealings.

The emphasis that anyone who wants to serve the Lord should be full of the Holy Spirit and wisdom sparked another yearning in him because as at that time, he was yet to receive the baptism of the Holy Spirit. He meditated extensively on the issue of good or honest reports. He thought of the impressions of others about him. He wondered what the reports would be if all of the brethren he had made contact or related with since he answered the altar call of salvation were to write about him. He determined to build a good relationship and reputation with believers and unbelievers alike without any compromise or sin. He remembered some of the Bible passages his mentor, Bro. Peter, shared with him on some Christian character traits as stated in Romans 12: 1-21.

It reads:
"Therefore I urge you, brothers and sisters, by the mercies of God, to present your bodies [dedicating all of yourselves, set apart] as a living sacrifice, holy and well-pleasing to God, which is your rational (logical, intelligent) act of worship. And do not be conformed to this world [any longer with its superficial values

and customs], but be transformed and progressively changed [as you mature spiritually] by the renewing of your mind [focusing on godly values and ethical attitudes], so that you may prove [for yourselves] what the will of God is, that which is good and acceptable and perfect [in His plan and purpose for you]. For by the grace [of God] given to me I say to every one of you not to think more highly of himself [and of his importance and ability] than he ought to think; but to think so as to have sound judgment, as God has apportioned to each a degree of faith [and a purpose designed for service]. For just as in one [physical] body we have many parts, and these parts do not all have the same function or special use, so we, who are many, are [nevertheless just] one body in Christ, and individually [we are] parts one of another [mutually dependent on each other]. Since we have gifts that differ according to the grace given to us, each of us is to use them accordingly: if [someone has the gift of] prophecy, [let him speak a new message from God to His people] in proportion to the faith possessed; if service, in the act of serving; or he who teaches, in the act of teaching; or he who encourages, in the act of encouragement; he who gives, with generosity; he who leads, with diligence; he who shows mercy [in caring for others], with cheerfulness. Love is to be sincere and active [the real thing— without guile and hypocrisy]. Hate what is evil [detest all ungodliness, do not tolerate wickedness]; hold on tightly to what is good. Be devoted to one another with [authentic] brotherly affection [as members of one family], give preference to one another in honor; never lagging behind in diligence; aglow in the Spirit, enthusiastically serving the Lord; constantly rejoicing in hope [because of our confidence in Christ], steadfast and patient in distress, devoted to prayer [continually seeking wisdom, guidance, and strength], contributing to the needs of God's people, pursuing [the practice of] hospitality. Bless those who persecute you [who cause you harm or hardship]; bless and do not curse [them]. Rejoice with those who rejoice [sharing others' joy], and weep with those who weep [sharing others' grief]. Live in harmony with one another; do not be haughty [conceited, self-important, exclusive], but associate with humble people [those with a realistic self-view]. Do not overestimate yourself. Never repay anyone evil for evil. Take thought for what is right and gracious and proper in the sight of everyone. If possible, as far as it depends on you, live at peace with everyone. Beloved, never avenge yourselves, but leave the way open for God's wrath [and His judicial righteousness]; for it is written [in Scripture], "VENGEANCE IS MINE, I WILL REPAY," says the Lord. "BUT IF YOUR ENEMY IS HUNGRY, FEED HIM; IF HE IS THIRSTY, GIVE HIM A DRINK; FOR BY DOING THIS YOU WILL HEAP BURNING COALS ON HIS HEAD." Do not be overcome and conquered by evil, but overcome evil with good."

Romans 14: 12-13. States:

"So then, each of us will give an account of himself to God. Then let us not criticize one another anymore, but rather determine this—not to put an obstacle or a stumbling block or a source of temptation in another believer's way."

Matthew. 7: 12 expresses:
""So then, in everything treat others the same way you want them to treat you, for this is [the essence of] the Law and the [writings of the] Prophets."
He was personally scared of Matthew. 18: 5-6:
"Whoever receives and welcomes one child like this in My name receives Me; but whoever causes one of these little ones who believe in Me to stumble and sin [by leading him away from My teaching], it would be better for him to have a heavy millstone [as large as one turned by a donkey] hung around his neck and to be drowned in the depth of the sea."

He derived great inspiration when he read John 14: 29-30. Jesus said: "I have told you now before it happen, so that when it does take place, you may believe and have faith [in Me]. I will not speak with you much longer, for the ruler of the world (Satan) is coming. And he has no claim on Me [no power over Me nor anything that he can use against Me];"

He desired to live to that expectation but he had the impression that, that was a personal testimony of Jesus and may not be humanly attainable. He took the

challenge to live up to John 14: 30 when he read the
account of Prophet Samuel, in 1Samuel. 12: 1-5. It
states:

"Then Samuel said to all Israel, "Behold, I have
listened to your voice in everything that you have said
to me and have appointed a king over you. And now,
here is the king walking before you. As for me, I am
old and gray, and here are my sons with you. I have
walked before you from my childhood to this day.
Here I am; testify against me before the LORD and
[Saul] His anointed [if I have done someone wrong].
Whose ox have I taken, or whose donkey have I taken,
or whom have I exploited? Whom have I oppressed or
from whose hand have I taken a bribe to blind my
eyes [to the truth]? [Tell me and] I will restore it to
you." They said, "You have not exploited us or
oppressed us or taken anything at all from a man's
hand." Samuel said to them, "The LORD is a witness
against you, and [Saul] His anointed is a witness this
day that you have not found anything in my hand."
And they answered, "He is a witness."

He concluded that integrity is a crucial aspect of
godliness through Christ. He was very inclined to be
able to say as Apostle Paul said:
"The things which you have learned and received and
heard and seen in me, practice these things [in daily

life], and the God [who is the source] of peace and well-being will be with you." Philippians 4:9 AMP

He read the admonition of Apostle Paul to Timothy stated in 2Timothy. 2:1-2.

"So you, my son, be strong [constantly strengthened] and empowered in the grace that is [to be found only] in Christ Jesus. The things [the doctrine, the precepts, the admonitions, the sum of my ministry] which you have heard me teach in the presence of many witnesses, entrust [as a treasure] to reliable and faithful men who will also be capable and qualified to teach others."

He could not get over the confidence and commendation of Apostle Paul as reflected in his letter to the brethren in Corinth.

"Imitate me, just as I imitate Christ. I praise and appreciate you because you remember me in everything and you firmly hold to the traditions [the substance of my instructions], just as I have passed them on to you." 1 Corinthians 11:1-2 AMP

He however realized his struggles. His knowledge of Apostle Paul's letter to the brethren in Rome, Romans, in the 7th and 8th chapters gave him a clue to what it takes to be a Christian with integrity and a defined calling. Relating with Romans 7: 18-25, he could not get over the first few verses of the 8th chapter which reads:

"Therefore there is now no condemnation [no guilty verdict, no punishment] for those who are in Christ Jesus [who believe in Him as personal Lord and Savior]. For the law of the Spirit of life [which is] in Christ Jesus [the law of our new being] has set you free from the law of sin and of death. For what the Law could not do [that is, overcome sin and remove its penalty, its power] being weakened by the flesh [man's nature without the Holy Spirit], God did: He sent His own Son in the likeness of sinful man as an offering for sin. And He condemned sin in the flesh [subdued it and overcame it in the person of His own Son], so that the [righteous and just] requirement of the Law might be fulfilled in us who do not live our lives in the ways of the flesh [guided by worldliness and our sinful nature], but [live our lives] in the ways of the Spirit [guided by His power]."
Romans 8:1-4 AMP

He developed a burning desire for the baptism of the Holy Spirit.

He read Matthew. 7: 7-11. Which states:
"Ask and keep on asking and it will be given to you; seek and keep on seeking and you will find; knock and keep on knocking and the door will be opened to you. For everyone who keeps on asking receives, and he who keeps on seeking finds, and to him who keeps on knocking, it will be opened. Or what man is there

among you who, if his son asks for bread, will [instead] give him a stone? Or if he asks for a fish, will [instead] give him a snake? If you then, evil (sinful by nature) as you are, know how to give good and advantageous gifts to your children, how much more will your Father who is in heaven [perfect as He is] give what is good and advantageous to those who keep on asking Him."

He was convinced beyond reasonable doubt that he will be fully baptized with the Holy Ghost. Recalling his experience on campus, when he went out for the laying on of hands for the baptism of the Holy Spirit, many of the brethren received the baptism which was evident by the individual's ability to speak in a new-tongue. He left the meeting with a little discouragement but with a consolation that it was the Holy Spirit that convicted him of sin and saved his soul through the blood of Jesus Christ. He could remember telling his friend Alfred, of blessed memory: "We have the Holy Spirit, but we are yet to be given the grace to speak in new tongues." Though his consolation sustained him, his consternation and mysteries of speaking a new tongue enhanced his yearning. His determination to abhor every form of sin was a great impetus to his encounter with the Holy Spirit. He had dreams and moments in the realm of the spirit when he found himself speaking in the Holy Ghost. On one particular occasion the expression in the Holy Ghost was very real and almost physically tangible. He was very sad when he opened his eyes only to realize it was an experience in his subconscious mind. His sorrow created a righteous indignation in him. He determined that every impediment to his speaking in the new tongue with his eyes open and his conscious mind at a full alert must be removed. He had a very deep burning desire for the presence of the Lord.

On a beautiful Sunday Morning, he was out to visit the president of his fellowship. He requested that they attend the nearest living church in the neighborhood. They arrived at a parish of Four Square Gospel Church. The preacher spoke as if he had every knowledge of Donald's struggles, consternation and aspirations. Concluding his sermon, he said: "If truly you have a desire for the encounter with the Holy Spirit and would want to be baptized of Him, today is your day." A session of prayers ensued.

Donald could not account for what actually happened to him. He just realized he could not speak any of the languages he had spoken in the past. He was rattling in an unknown tongue. Though aware of his environment, he was captivated by the power that suppressed his logic and rationalization. The service was over but he was still on his knees at the rear of the church. He wanted to cut-off but he could not until he felt a release. When he opened his eyes, he saw his fellowship president who played host to him for the glorious weekend that was to usher him into the propelling force of his calling. He felt a "voltage of power" running through him. He could not explain the feelings. He felt lightness in his entire body. He conclusively said to himself: "I believe 'Cardo' is dead and the true Donald created by the Lord has been redeemed and endowed with the divine nature." He joyfully recited:

"I have been crucified with Christ [that is, in Him I have shared His crucifixion]; it is no longer I who live, but Christ lives in me. The life I now live in the body I live by faith [by adhering to, relying on, and completely trusting] in the Son of God, who loved me and gave Himself up for me." Galatians 2:20 AMP

"Therefore there is now no condemnation [no guilty verdict, no punishment] for those who are in Christ Jesus [who believe in Him as personal Lord and Savior]. For the law of the Spirit of life [which is] in Christ Jesus [the law of our new being] has set you free from the law of sin and of death."
Romans 8:1-2 AMP

He felt he was ready to take up any God-given spiritual assignment from the Lord. He remembered one of his sessions with his mentor and pastor, when in response to his question he was told: "The Lord does not use compulsion on his willing children but may be compelled to use some tough measures against His beloved but recalcitrant and disobedient children or messengers. Like He did to Jonah, Balam, Samson, Saul of Tarsus..."

He was ready to hearken to divine instructions. He went to his pastor for some guidance on crucial issues of his life. His pastor was able to see his eagerness, readiness and the radiance of the glory of God upon his life. He said to him: "I guess I have recognized you in this church for quite some years now. I have noticed some great changes in you of late. I was first stunned by your stand on some issues during the Sunday school sessions some months back. I hope I will not be embarrassing you if I ask you whether you noticed a change in your personal desires, passion and values." With a broad smile Donald briefly narrated all that he had passed through in the past almost three years. His pastor was very thrilled and impressed.

Staring at his face, the pastor said: "There is no doubt that the Lord has prepared you for some great tasks in the ministry. May I ask about your areas of interest since you gave your life to Jesus? What are the areas of ministry that you feel you can be used of the Lord to infuse a higher level of performance or spiritual sanity? What do you have burning desires for...? As good as my questions may sound, the Lord may choose to lay some ideas or areas of ministry in your heart such that others or you have never thought or dreamt of." With a deep sigh, he responded, Sir, I guess I have to spend some time in prayers to come to a final conclusion. Though I currently function in some aspects of the church, I cannot say with all assurance and conviction that I have a specific calling of the Lord for my life. However, I am ready to serve." He concluded.

The pastor encouraged him to read: Ephesians 4:10-13, 1Corinthians. 12: 7-12, before he engages in his planned prayers. They were about to part but the pastor insisted that they should first read the text. He took his Bible and read:

"He who descended is the very same as He who also has ascended high above all the heavens, that He [His presence] might fill all things [that is, the whole universe]). And [His gifts to the church were varied and] He Himself appointed some as apostles [special messengers, representatives], some as prophets [who speak a new message from God to the people], some as evangelists [who spread the good news of salvation], and some as pastors and teachers [to shepherd and guide and instruct], [and He did this] to fully equip and perfect the saints (God's people) for works of service, to build up the body of Christ [the church]; until we all reach oneness in the faith and in the knowledge of the Son of God, [growing spiritually] to become a mature believer, reaching to the measure

of the fullness of Christ [manifesting His spiritual completeness and exercising our spiritual gifts in unity]. So that we are no longer children [spiritually immature], tossed back and forth [like ships on a stormy sea] and carried about by every wind of [shifting] doctrine, by the cunning and trickery of [unscrupulous] men, by the deceitful scheming of people ready to do anything [for personal profit]."
Ephesians 4:10-14 AMP

"But to each one is given the manifestation of the Spirit [the spiritual illumination and the enabling of the Holy Spirit] for the common good. To one is given through the [Holy] Spirit [the power to speak] the message of wisdom, and to another [the power to express] the word of knowledge and understanding according to the same Spirit; to another [wonder-working] faith [is given] by the same [Holy] Spirit, and to another the [extraordinary] gifts of healings by the one Spirit; and to another the working of miracles, and to another prophecy [foretelling the future, speaking a new message from God to the people], and to another discernment of spirits [the ability to distinguish sound, godly doctrine from the deceptive doctrine of man-made religions and cults], to another various kinds of [unknown] tongues, and to another interpretation of tongues. All these things [the gifts, the achievements, the abilities, the empowering] are brought about by one and the same [Holy] Spirit, distributing to each one individually just as He chooses. For just as the body is one and yet have many parts, and all the parts, though many, form [only] one body, so it is with Christ."1 Corinthians 12:7-12 AMP

It was not too difficult for the pastor to conclude that Donald had a pastoral calling. By now he had been the youth leader of the church for over a year. He started a thriving fellowship at his local station where he worked as a teacher in one of the high schools. His role in leadership as a youth in the church had tremendous impact on all the youths and the entire church. He led the regional evangelistic outreach program as directed by the national body of the church. He was instrumental to the purchase of the church van used to convey his converts from the village to the church in the city. He was the foremost interpreter for the pastor in their Sunday services. However, the pastor was reluctant to send him out to pioneer a parish of the church. The membership of his converts in the village where he was a teacher grew to a point that the van will necessarily have to travel twice on a Sunday to convey them. He was very faithful to his attendance of the youth meetings and workers preparatory meetings that took place on Saturdays. The pastor, after the workers meeting on one of the Saturdays, informed him that the church van will no longer be able to come to his village to convey the brethren to worship in the city. He was encouraged to pastor the converts. Donald was shocked. He tried to explain to the pastor why he was not qualified or capable to lead a congregation. The pastor walked away from him. He had no choice but to carry out the instruction of his spiritual father.

He was wondering whether that was the implication, interpretation or meaning of a revelation he had. He saw himself interpreting for his father in the Lord, Gabriel O'Far and suddenly he was teleported to a different location. He was the preacher with someone interpreting for him. In his assumption, it was like a play-back of his experience with his former Sunday-school teacher Grace Ajor under Pastor Gabriel O'Far. When he took a teaching job in a school, seventy miles from the Church. He told him: "Go and grow where you are planted". That was how he had to come to the nearest parish of same church under the pastoral care of Pastor Rufus in Rock City. He came to a conclusion that God probably was calling him to pastoral ministry. He was not nursing the ambition of becoming a pastor. He was pleased with being a faithful brother in ministry with liberty to practice his most treasured skill of being an artist.

On the following Sunday morning, the converts gathered together, waiting for the arrival of the Church van. He called them into his sitting room and informed them of the Pastor's decision. He preached his first sermon with someone interpreting for him. He could not imagine himself in the pastoral calling.

Few weeks later, he went to his pastor for a feedback on their previous discussions, especially on the subject of identifying his calling. The discussion was brief. His pastor informed him that in his own conviction, he [Donald] was already operating in his calling as a pastor prior to their discussion. He called his attention to his lines of actions as previously narrated. "Remember you told me that you fast at least two and a half days every week. You have made evangelism and discipleship your mandatory task. You have been an adherent to the Christian rites, rituals and dogmas. I have made a good analysis of your person for some time now. I was only reluctant to release you into the pastoral ministry because you are not yet married. I considered the dangers and temptations pastors face with 'grateful women'."

Considering the number of matured ladies in your youth group in the church and the ones you won to the Lord in your local station, I considered it necessary to release you into what I believe is your calling. With a deep breath, he affirmed that his pastor believed he was called to be a pastor. "I agree with you on that, "his Pastor asserted.

Reacting to his pastor's, he said: "I believe that the Lord has called me into marriage ministry. I have been very concerned about what is going on amongst the singles and the married people. I felt the Lord needs me to impact them." "I very much agree with you on that note also. The marriage ministry is a subsidiary of your calling as a pastor. Just remain focused on the

Lord to avoid the temptations in the Pastoral Ministry."

In his closing remarks, he read:
"Therefore let the one who thinks he stands firm [immune to temptation, being overconfident and self-righteous], take care that he does not fall [into sin and condemnation]. No temptation [regardless of its source] has overtaken or enticed you that is not common to human experience [nor is any temptation unusual or beyond human resistance]; but God is faithful [to His word—He is compassionate and trustworthy], and He will not let you be tempted beyond your ability [to resist], but along with the temptation He [has in the past and is now and] will [always] provide the way out as well, so that you will be able to endure it [without yielding, and will overcome temptation with joy]. Therefore, my beloved, run [keep far, far away] from [any sort of] idolatry [and that includes loving anything more than God, or participating in anything that leads to sin and enslaves the soul]. I am speaking as to wise and sensible people; judge [carefully and thoughtfully consider] for yourselves what I say."
1 Corinthians 10:12-15 AMP

Finally, he cautioned him: "Do your best to avoid temptations. They will surely come, but you can reduce or disarm them by the grace of God and your personal comportment."

Integrity is a crucial aspect of godliness
through Christ. Be a worthy ambassador.

CHAPTER THREE

TEMPTATIONS IN MINISTERIAL CALLINGS

Every one that is called would be made by the one who called him or her into the ministry. Jesus told the would-be disciplined:" Follow Me [as My disciples, accepting me as your Master and Teacher and walking the same path of life that I walk], and I will make you fishers of men."" Matthew 4:19b AMP

To 'make' in this context means to be schooled, instructed, enriched, empowered, granted liberty, bring into the fullness of life, liberated from all negativities.

The making starts from the moment of response to the call. Calling is the evidence of divine acceptance and approval in anticipation of maximization of endowment. God does not call the indolent into ministry. A momentary inactivity does not imply indolence. Moments of inactivity may always be a moment for good reflection in anticipation of a better performance. Nathaniel, who was recruited by the

Lord Jesus, was found sitting under a tree. He was not necessarily indolent, neither was he insolent for the question he asked about the person of Jesus. His response was evident of spiritual ignorance based on his personal integrity and readiness to serve. These were the attributes that qualified him for recruitment by the master.

The Bible states:
"Philip found Nathanael and told him, "We have found the One Moses in the Law and also the Prophets wrote about—Jesus from Nazareth, the son of Joseph [according to public record]." Nathanael answered him, "Can anything good come out of Nazareth?" Philip replied, "Come and see." Jesus saw Nathanael coming toward Him, and said of him, "Here is an Israelite indeed [a true descendant of Jacob], in whom there is no guile nor deceit nor duplicity!" Nathanael said to Jesus, "How do You know [these things about] me?" Jesus answered, "Before Philip called you, when you were still under the fig tree, I saw you." Nathanael answered, "Rabbi (Teacher), You are the Son of God; You are the King of Israel." Jesus replied, "Because I said to you that I saw you under the fig tree, do you believe [in Me]? You will see greater things than this." Then He said to him, "I assure you and most solemnly say to you, you will see heaven opened and the angels of God ascending and descending on the Son of Man [the bridge between heaven and earth]."
John 1:45-51 AMP

Most of the "called" were vessels unto honor in the presence of the Lord. Their callings were based on spiritual accountability which enhanced their acceptance, not their human ability. The fact remains as evident by facts of history that vessels chosen by God are always the target of the devil. He does not make cheap choices. Nonentities are of no concern to him. He counts his time and strength very precious and would not be dissipated on valueless personalities. He targets the "Spiritual Giants," whose fall he believes would discourage, derail or derange others. This is the very reason why every spiritual leader should not trivialize the spirituality of their calling.

Prophet Samuel said to King Saul:
"Is it not true that even though you were small (insignificant) in your own eyes, you were made the head of the tribes of Israel? And the LORD anointed you king over Israel, and the LORD sent you on a mission, and said, 'Go, totally destroy the sinners, the Amalekites, and fight against them until they are eliminated.' Why did you not obey the voice of the LORD, but [instead] swooped down on the plunder [with shouts of victory] and did evil in the sight of the LORD?" 1Samuel 15:17-19 AMP

Most of the fallen leaders started well but were corrupted in the course of their services to the Lord. They were victims of the deceitfulness of sin. They trivialized the spirituality of their office. There is no doubt that if sin appears in its true color, no reasonable person will fall a victim of its antics. The camouflage of sin is similar to the packaging of the capsules by the pharmacists. The capsule has a bitter content that is encapsulated by a thin film. Victims of sin are blinded and not able to realize that sin is a killer. Satan does not have any greater access to human spirit than through the human flesh; the lustful desires. Jesus said:

"It is the Spirit who gives life; the flesh conveys no benefit [it is of no account]. The words I have spoken to you are spirit and life [providing eternal life]."
John 6:63 AMP

The subject of calling has been of great concern to Donald since he read Apostle Paul's letter to the Philippians:

"However, I thought it necessary to send back to you Epaphroditus, [who has been] my brother and companion and fellow soldier, who was also sent as your messenger to take care of my needs. For he has been longing for all of you and was distressed because you had heard that he was sick. He certainly was sick and close to death. But God had mercy on him, and not only on him but also on me, so that I would not have sorrow upon sorrow. So I have sent him all the more eagerly so that when you see him again you may rejoice and I may be less concerned about you. Welcome him home in the Lord with great joy, and appreciate and honor men like him; because he came close to death for the work of Christ, risking his life to complete what was lacking in your service to me [which distance prevented you from rendering personally]." Philippians 2:25-30 AMP

He feared the associated challenges with commitments to ministry. He had realized that it is a call to selfless services and dreadful challenges. He lived in constant self-examination of his sincerity to the calling to pastoral ministry as expressed by his pastor. He had no reason to doubt the fact that he derived joy in discipleship but was not sure whether he was ready for the experience of Epaphroditus.

He saw the calling into pastoral ministry as a test of his dependency on God to cope with human needs, differences and idiosyncrasies. He had listened and learned a lot from his pastor. He had no reason to doubt the doctrinal standard of his pastor but was anxious to read and learn from other writers or preachers on the social media. He was very skeptical of the messages and doctrines of many of the preachers. He approached his pastor for guidance. He wanted to know the books and preachers that had influenced his own life in the ministry. His pastor was very impressed that he was ready to learn, especially through reading of books in the age where many Christians have become very lazy at reading. Not many were ready to read for spiritual enlightenment but for financial and material betterment. His pastor had no doubt that Donald would excel above his contemporaries. He recommended books from various authors which included but not limited to the following:

Charles Finney, Kenneth Copeland, Kenneth Hagins, E.A. Adeboye, Oral Robert...

He gave him a very great caution on the aspect of listening to preachers on the internet and other social media. He mentioned to him some of the preachers he had heard preaching what he believed to be heresies and very misleading. At the close of the discussion, Donald asked a pertinent question: "Sir, you have been in the pastoral ministry for over forty years. Can you please tell me the secret of your sustenance?" His pastor looked into his eyes and said: "Minister Donald, I realize you are ready to learn and get all you can from every reliable source on the subject of the kingdom. Today has been a very busy day for us both. I want to assure you that by the grace of God I will do my best to make the best of your readiness to learn. You do not have to be in a hurry. I may be aged but not about to go home yet. The Lord will surely spare me to have time to impart and impact people like you who are being prepared for the coming generation.

The secret of my survival in the ministry has been the grace of God that enabled me to abstain from sin. With a broad smile he pulled him to himself as he prayed: "Father I thank you for this hungry soul that you have brought into my life to fulfill purpose in this generation and those to come. I pray for your son that he will not disappoint you; those of us who have seen your light in him. He will not disappoint himself in the mighty name of Jesus Christ. Father, please let this your son have a better experience in the ministry. I pray that you grant him successes in the areas where I have missed the mark. Father, please let him accomplish in good time those things that took us ages to achieve. Please let this your son be greater than me in the ministry. Father I pray, your son shall be a pillar of righteousness in your house. Thank you Father for this privilege; in Jesus's name we have prayed. "Donald responded with a very resounding AMEN."

As they parted, Donald wondered on the content of the prayers of his pastor for him. He was a little agitated by the aspect: "Please let this your son be greater than me in the ministry." He could not imagine how he would in any area of ministry be greater than his pastor. He was a little scared when he thought of the challenges associated with the leadership of big ministries. He remembered one of his pastor's sermons on the avoidance of sin. In the sermon, he put sin into three categories called the "3Gs": Glory, Gold and Gender.

GLORY: A desire to be seen as having the power or ability to solve the problems of the people. Attributing to oneself the power of divine enablement.

GOLD: A desire to have abundance of money for the attainment of lofty heights for self-aggrandizement.

GENDER: A desire for inordinate sexual fulfillment with opposite sex.

He laughed when he remembered what his pastor called "The demonic instinct" that gravitates people of same sex towards each other. According to him, wild animals are more sensible than the homosexuals. He soliloquized: "My pastor told me to preserve whatever defines me and destroy whatever will devour me".

He was overwhelmed by the fall of some ministers in recent time. In his assessment, sexual related sins were the principal causes of the fall of many of the ministers. He wondered why adultery and fornication are the pitfalls of many Christians including young and aging ministers of the gospel. He was extremely sensitive to any move of the opposite sex. He was always skeptical of some men that make suspicious moves that suggest undue intimacies. He lamented over the fall of Pastor Davidson, a victim of sexual promiscuity. He determined to solicit the help of his pastor to work on his [Davidson] restoration.

Pastor Rufus was excited to see Donald walk into his office. He was ready to listen to and answer some inquisitive questions on burning desire for his personal spiritual growth. The pastor was a little surprised that he came around just to plead that something be done on efforts to restore fallen Pastor Davidson. "Thank you for your concern for our beloved Pastor Davidson. I know that the news of his fall has been the talk of the town. He was not well received by all for his integrity before his fall. His notoriety had been blown out of proportion by the devil. It's all attempts of the devil to cast aspersions on the name of the Lord and Christianity in general. Efforts had been made to reach out to him, but he has not been cooperative. He has been completely estranged by the devil. He saw everyone that went to see him as an enemy of what he claimed to be his compliance with the instruction that he got from the Lord." "The Lord?" Donald interrupted. "I guess you need to know the genesis of the unfortunate saga of the devil," pastor Rufus inferred. "Sir, how did it happen or let me say how did Pastor Davidson degenerate to this awkward and embarrassing level?"

"Yes, I believe that young ministers like you need to learn from the experience of those of us who have seen more days than you in the ministry. Pastor Davidson was a very fervent minister of the gospel. I am sure you knew him for his gentle disposition. He however had a hidden flair for ladies. How I wish he had confessed this to notable ministers that would have helped him out through deliverance. His mentor had so much confidence in him and would least suspect the hidden "JOKER-CARD" which the devil kept in place for his destruction, almost at the zenith of his attainment in the ministry. There was a rumor raised against him of similar incident many years ago, but no one could authenticate the allegations. How I wished he learnt his lesson as at then and abstained from such a practice. The fact is that those who get involved in illicit sexual relationship are held captive by the devil until the appointed time of their destruction. How I wish ministers of the gospel would realize that they were coopted into spiritual assignments while they live on earth. May I advise you to keep to one salient caution of my mother which she repeatedly chanted to my hearing when I was growing up. She would always warn me and caution thus: "Don't attempt a vice. Don't play the ostrich. Abstinence is the best resolve."

Apostle Paul wrote:
"Abstain from every form of evil [withdraw and keep away from it]. Now may the God of peace Himself sanctify you through and through [that is, separate you from profane and vulgar things, make you pure and whole and undamaged—consecrated to Him—set apart for His purpose]; and may your spirit and soul and body be kept complete and [be found] blameless at the coming of our Lord Jesus Christ."
1 Thessalonians 5:22-23 AMP

With an expression of grief, Donald said: "Sir, I am sorry to ask whether you have really prayed for the deliverance of Pastor Davidson" "Yes! we prayed and fasted for him. We visited him. I am personally devastated and frustrated; I do not know what and how to talk to him anymore on this issue. He uses the Bible to defend his evil actions. He claimed David had many wives. Solomon was not condemned for having over a thousand women in his life. He emphatically referred to Prophet Hosea's relationship with a harlot. His claims deflated my zeal. It became very difficult for me to meet with him again on the issue. He almost made me see God as a tolerant God who would not punish sin. Though I had my evidence to believe that he was already under the judgement of God as he lost his ministry and confidence reposed in him by the brethren. I am getting to understand the implication of Hebrews. 6: 4-6:

"For [it is impossible to restore to repentance] those who have once been enlightened [spiritually] and who have tasted and consciously experienced the heavenly gift and have shared in the Holy Spirit, and have tasted and consciously experienced the good word of God and the powers of the age (world) to come, and then have fallen away—it is impossible to bring them back again to repentance, since they again nail the Son of God on the cross [for as far as they are concerned, they are treating the death of Christ as if they were not saved by it], and are holding Him up again to public disgrace."

I promise to continue to pray for him, but I do not feel comfortable going to dialogue with him. I am very cautious of the maintenance of my personal spiritual sanity. Please, pay serious attention to this statement of Apostle Paul:

"Brothers, if anyone is caught in any sin, you who are spiritual [that is, you who are responsive to the guidance of the Spirit] are to restore such a person in a spirit of gentleness [not with a sense of superiority or self-righteousness], keeping a watchful eye on yourself, so that you are not tempted as well."
Galatians 6:1 AMP

"I guess he has become hardened by the devil. Remember the statement of Apostle Paul to Timothy:
"But the [Holy] Spirit explicitly and unmistakably declares that in later times some will turn away from the faith, paying attention instead to deceitful and seductive spirits and doctrines of demons, [misled] by the hypocrisy of liars whose consciences are seared as with a branding iron [leaving them incapable of ethical functioning]," 1 Timothy 4:1-2 AMP

"Though I still have a great concern for Pastor Davidson, I am however more concerned about people like you that are coming up in the ministerial callings.

May I advise that on your own, you find time to read the following Bible texts: Ezra 4:11-18, Jeremiah. 2: 32, Jeremiah 13: 23-27, Hebrews. 3:10-14. Psalm 137, Hebrews. 10: 22-27. Jeremiah 2:31-37, Jeremiah 3:21-23, Jeremiah. 4: 1-4. With a stern look, he said, "Promise me that you will read these texts." "Sir, I promise," Donald responded.

It was time for them to part. Pastor Rufus would have as usual led a session of prayers. He did not show any intent. It was a test of the spirituality of Donald and how much he believed in the spiritual leadership of his pastor and mentor. "Sir, please pray for me before I leave." With a heartfelt joy, Pastor Rufus prayed for his mentee. In his prayers, he conclusively said: "Father, have mercy on us all that we may finish well and strong. Please count us worthy to spend eternity with you in heaven, in Jesus' mighty name. Donald shouted a resounding Amen.

He could not rest until he had read the Bible passages given to him by his pastor. He ruminated on the contents of the passages and came to a resolute decision that he will not grant the devil any foothold in his life. He could not get over the Lord's statement in Jeremiah 4: 4

"Circumcise (dedicate, sanctify) yourselves to the LORD And remove the foreskin [sins] of your heart, Men of Judah and inhabitants of Jerusalem, Or else

My wrath will go forth like fire [consuming all that gets in its way] And burn and there will be no one to quench it, Because of the evil of your acts."

He was a little agitated when he made a fair assessment of the moves of one of the young ladies in his youth group at the mother-church. She had visited him twice in his local station. Though his relationship with her had been platonic. He realized that he was fairly sexually aroused during her second visit. He could not really advance a good reason why he should suspect the lady for his personal sexual arousal. He conclusively decided to inform the lady not to visit him alone and without prior information. He determined to do that to avoid any exposure to temptation.

It was the tradition of A-Z Holiness church that all newly established parishes should return their tithe and offering to the mother-church while they are given some funds for the upkeep of the church. Pastor Donald's church was young and sizable memberships of the church were high school students. He was convinced that the Lord was leading him to acquire a piece of land for the building of the permanent site for the church. He was going to build his personal house in the village before the Lord directed him to divert all the efforts to the construction of a church in the village. He was categorically informed that his personal house was not going to be in the village. This information was given to him in his prayer session. He rose from his knees, dressed up and headed for the city to inform his senior pastor and mentor about the voice of the Lord. He went straight to his pastor so that the devil or his personal desires would not change the spiritual conviction that he should hand over his personal project to the Lord. In no time, the church building construction started and was completed in record time.

The news of his building a Church spread like a plague. Many of his friends and extended family members mocked and ridiculed him for spending his time and money on the church. There was an occasion when a funeral was to be conducted in a nearby village. Many of his friends and extended family members were present. Some of them drove through the village where he resided but none of them checked on him. He was to be there, but he had no car of his own to drive on the rough and dusty road that led to the village. He pleaded with the driver of a double cabin pickup truck to give him a ride to the village where the funeral rites were to take place. Though he was going to pay for the trip, the only available space was the open back of the truck. He had no choice as he was desperate to get to the venue. He rode with them. At the end of the journey, he was fully covered with dust. His outfit had taken another color. He did his best to clean off the dust but to no avail. It was obvious that he rode through terrible dust. His friends who had gotten there before him greeted him sarcastically and charged him for spending his money on the construction of a church. They showed him their cars and asked why he did not have one, though they knew the probable reason.

On leaving the funeral ceremony, Donald was very sad and discouraged. The devil taunted him. He was tempted to align with the proposals of his friends on "making money" and "enjoying life" so as it were. At this juncture, the Lord whispered to his soul: "BE WATCHFUL, DON'T BE TEMPTED TO LEAVE JESUS". It was almost an audible voice. The caution sank deep into his Spirit-man. As an artist, he designed a nicely illustrated poster design. The design sold like hot cake. It was a propelling force to the fulfillment of his destiny. He felt very happy that he did not fall into the temptation of money. He remembered one of the quotable quotes of his pastor: "Money should never be granted the right of becoming the determinant of value. Wherever or whenever money becomes the determinant of value, insincerity becomes inevitable".

Lucifer does not make a cheap choice and does not let go his potential highly placed victims. Donald was always shown the glory of the possessions of the childhood friends and extended family members. He was very down on one occasion but was beautifully counseled by Pastor Kenny Abbey who was attached to his local church on his internship from the Bible College. He told him that any time he [Donald] feels down, he should go to the church, walk round and have a good look at the beautiful edifice. The counsel worked as a very effective therapy of encouragement to pull him out of any depression, torment or temptations. The statement of his pastor that "abstinence is the best resolve" and "the scar is never like the skin" became his great caution against sin.

CHAPTER FOUR

THE FALL INTO SIN

Temptation is not a sin but a lead-way to sin and destruction. Many that fell into sin did so because they lingered too long with temptation. Resisting temptation is a show of strength, avoiding temptation is a display of wisdom. It is important to realize that strength may fail but keeping the distance makes you play safe. The fall into sin is determined by the thought life of the individual. The climax of a negative thought-life is the breeding ground of sin. Whether an accidental fall or a deliberate act of sin, the die is cast, the deal done, the dent becomes evident and the consequence cannot be ignored.

No individual lives a better life than his or her thought-life. The Bible instructs every would-be successful Christian on what to think about:

"Finally, believers, whatever is true, whatever is honorable and worthy of respect, whatever is right and confirmed by God's word, whatever is pure and wholesome, whatever is lovely and brings peace, whatever is admirable and of good repute; if there is

any excellence, if there is anything worthy of praise, think continually on these things [center your mind on them, and implant them in your heart]."
Philippians 4:8 AMP

Sin is never an accident but is the consequence of negative thoughts, habits, practices and life-style.
Apostle John wrote:

"The one who practices sin [separating himself from God, and offending Him by acts of disobedience, indifference, or rebellion] is of the devil [and takes his inner character and moral values from him, not God]; for the devil has sinned and violated God's law from the beginning. The Son of God appeared for this purpose, to destroy the works of the devil. No one who is born of God [deliberately, knowingly, and habitually] practices sin, because God's seed [His principle of life, the essence of His righteous character] remains [permanently] in him [who is born again—who is reborn from above—spiritually transformed, renewed, and set apart for His purpose]; and he [who is born again] cannot habitually [live a life characterized by] sin, because he is born of God and longs to please Him." 1 John 3:8-9 AMP

Donald as an ardent listener to good Christian speakers and addicted reader of good literatures, in most cases acted balance on issues of the Christian faith. His moral standard superseded that of his contemporaries. He was a darling to many notable ministers and a pared-leader-figure to his colleagues.

He spent most of his time studying the scriptures. In his studies of the book of Judges, he was able to see in the scriptures, at least eight reasons for the fall of Samson.

1]. Ignorance and negligence of divine mandate.

2]. Breach of divine principles.

3]. Given to anger.

4]. Contempt of divine instructions.

5]. Abuse of power.

6]. Toying with sin.

7]. Mistaking lust for love.

8]. Vengeance and irreversibility.

IGNORANCE AND NEGLIGENCE OF DIVINE MANDATE

Prior to the conception of Samson, the angel of the Lord gave the parents, precisely the mother, instructions and mandate concerning the conception, birth and life of Samson.

The Bible states:

"And the Angel of the LORD appeared to the woman and said to her, "Behold, you are infertile and have no children, but you shall conceive and give birth to a son. Therefore, be careful not to drink wine or [any other] intoxicating drink, and do not eat anything [ceremonially] unclean. For behold, you shall conceive and give birth to a son. No razor shall come upon his head, for the boy shall be a Nazirite [dedicated] to

God from birth; and he shall begin to rescue Israel from the hands of the Philistines."
Judges 13:3-5 AMP

The Bible did not categorically or emphatically record that Samson was well instructed on the principles or instructions of God about his life. If he was well tutored on the rules and the purpose of his life, he must have been negligent to have allowed or fallen victim of many of the errors.

BREACH OF DIVINE PRINCIPLES

According to the divine instruction given to Moses on the account of the children of Israel, a Nazarite should not touch a dead body. The Bible was emphatic on this issue. It was to be taken as a very serious injunction. It would be wrong for him to touch the dead body of his parents or relatives even in the agony of their death. He was not to touch the dead body of an animal that was not properly slaughtered. This was why the Levites were no hunters or archers as described in the Bible. Biblical record stated that Samson killed a young lion that roared at him on his way to Tim-nath. After a while, he returned and took honey from the carcass of the lion.
"So he scraped the honey out into his hands and went on, eating as he went. When he came to his father and mother, he gave them some, and they ate it; but he did not tell them he had taken the honey from the body of the lion." Judges 14:9 AMP

GIVEN TO ANGER

Anger is a destroyer of both the assailed and the assailant. It is a hidden weapon of the devil against its victim. It cost Moses access to the Promised Land. Samson like others, did not learn from history. He fell a victim of anger after his betrothed wife was used by the Philistines to decipher his riddle. The Bible states: "So the men of the city said to Samson on the seventh day before sundown, "What is sweeter than honey? What is stronger than a lion?" And he said to them, "If you had not plowed with my heifer, You would not have solved my riddle." Then the Spirit of the LORD came upon him mightily, and he went down to Ashkelon and killed thirty of them and took their gear, and gave changes of clothes to those who had explained the riddle. And his anger burned, and he went up to his father's house. But Samson's wife was given to his companion who had been his friend."
Judges 14:18-20 AMP

His impetuous anger made him forget about his betrothed wife for a good stretch of time that gave his prospective in-law the impression that he detested her. Anger opened him up to other vices.

CONTEMPT OF DIVINE INSTRUCTION

Samson was conscious of the presence of God in his life. He should have known that it was not expedient for him to go into a harlot or a prostitute. He was contemptuous against God.

The Bible states:

"Then Samson went to Gaza and saw a prostitute there, and went in to her. The Gazites were told, "Samson has come here." So they surrounded the place and waited all night at the gate of the city to ambush him. They kept quiet all night, saying, "In the morning, when it is light, we will kill him."
JUDGES 16: 1-2

He showed no remorse for his transgression. One would have thought he ought to realize he did something wrong and therefore seek the face of the Lord for forgiveness. Instead, he rested in sleep till midnight.

THE ABUSE OF POWER
When Samson woke up from his sleep after a promiscuous act with a prostitute, he was not repentant but went on to exercise the power of God. The Bible states:

"But Samson lay [resting] until midnight, then at midnight he got up and took hold of the doors of the city gate and the two door-posts, and pulled them up; [security] bar and all, and he put them on his shoulders and carried them up to the top of the hill which is opposite Hebron." Judges 16:3 AMP

These actions of Samson reveal the danger inherent in the assertion of Apostle Paul:

"For the gifts and the calling of God are irrevocable [for He does not withdraw what He has given, nor does He change His mind about those to whom He gives His grace or to whom He sends His call]."
Romans 11:29 AMP

God may honor his word or carry out his intention even when "the called" is operating in sin or blatant disobedience to divine instruction. Just like Moses and Aron did in the book of Numbers.

"...Moses and Aaron gathered the assembly before the rock. Moses said to them, "Listen now, you rebels; must we bring you water out of this rock?" Then Moses raised his hand [in anger] and with his rod he struck the rock twice [instead of speaking to the rock as the LORD had commanded]. And the water poured out abundantly, and the congregation and their livestock drank [fresh water]. But the LORD said to Moses and Aaron, "Because you have not believed (trusted) Me, to treat Me as holy in the sight of the sons of Israel, you therefore shall not bring this assembly into the land which I have given them.""
Numbers 20:10-12 AMP

A TOYING WITH SIN

Samson fell in "love" with a lady called Delilah. She was mandated by the leaders of the Philistines to find out the secret of his power. The lady was direct in her request but Samson was careless and insensitive. He had lost his bearing with the calling of God upon his life.

"So Delilah said to Samson, "Please tells me where your great strength lies and with what you may be bound and subdued."Judges 16:6 AMP

Samson told her series of lies on the secret of his power. Her several attempts on his destruction were enough for any reasonable person to refrain from such a path. He was to be a victim of the consequence of toying with sin. He was a victim of lust.

MISTAKEN LUST FOR LOVE

It is a common saying that, "LOVE IS BLIND" Others say: "Love was said to be born blind but "REALITIES" opened its eyes." The truth is that it is LUST that is unreasonably blind. If Samson was realistic and not lustful and unreasonably blinded, he must have realized that his calling and his life were at stake while he was toying with sin in his dialogue with Delilah. "Then she said to him, "How can you say, 'I love you,' when your heart is not with me? You have mocked me these three times and have not told me where your great strength lies." When she pressured him day after day with her words and pleaded with him, he was annoyed to death. Then [finally] he told her everything that was in his heart and said to her, "A razor has never been used on my head, for I have been a Nazirite to God from my mother's womb. If I am shaved, then my strength will leave me, and I will become weak and be like any [other] man."
Judges 16:15-17 AMP

Samson was completely betrayed by his lustful life, which sold him into the hands of Delilah and the lords of the Philistines. He paid a terrible price for taking God for granted. The Bible states:

"She made Samson sleep on her knees, and she called a man and had him shave off the seven braids of his head. Then she began to abuse Samson, and his strength left him. She said, "The Philistines are upon you, Samson!" And he awoke from his sleep and said, "I will go out as I have time after time and shake myself free." For Samson did not know that the LORD had departed from him. Then the Philistines seized him and gouged out his eyes; and they brought him down to Gaza and bound him with [two] bronze chains; and he was forced to be a grinder [of grain into flour at the mill] in the prison." Judges 16:19-21 AMP

There was no doubt Samson had violated the most divine instructions. He must have been very-well drunken when the seven locks on his head were being shaven. He was used to spiritual indulgences. Indulgence was never a mark of love but a bait of destruction. He did not realize that the Spirit of the Lord had departed from him. Whenever the devil wins over a minister of the Lord, the first line of action is to destroy the vision and send the individual into servitude.

VENGEANCE AND IRREVERSIBILITY

In most cases the wounded are vengeful. This is the root of un-forgiveness which eventually could lead the individual into self-destruction. Such people always have the belief that their lines of thoughts are irreversible.

God gave Samson a second chance to regain all he had lost. His perception and line of thought was the actual cause of his death. He requested that he might die with the Philistines. If he had requested that he should live after he had destroyed his enemies, God would have kept him alive. He was unable to forgive the Philistines neither was he able to forgive himself. The Bible states:

"But the hair of his head began to grow again after it had been shaved off."

And Samson said, "Let me die with the Philistines!" And he stretched out with all his might [collapsing the support pillars], and the house fell on the lords and on all the people who were in it. So the dead whom he killed at his death were more than those whom he had killed during his life." Judges 16:22, 30 AMP

The truth is that he had lost bearing with his calling. If he had valued the spirituality of his calling above the vindication of himself, he would have prayed for restoration and the fulfillment of his purpose.

The life and ministry of Samson were cut short due to licentiousness, trivialities, anger and vindictiveness.

Donald was cautious of his personal comportment especially in connection with his calling in the ministry. He had heard his pastor say that: "There is no one that actually falls into sin without firstly walking into sin." He determined never to toy with, walk into or walk with sin.

He had learnt a great lesson from the fall of his one-time mentor, Pastor Jimmy. He made up his mind never to be lured into undue relationship with any lady, either physically or through the internet. Pastor Jimmy was infatuated by pornographic pictures and videos. He eventually got addicted, until he got into the real act of sexual promiscuity. He degenerated into harlotry with "call-girls" and was trapped by the media. He was recorded on video in one of his illicit relationship with a "call-girl." He lost his fame and ministry. There were diverse calls for sympathy in various quarters. Others felt he was a disappointment to the circle of the clergy. Many agreed he should be forgiven. Obviously, the scar is never like the skin. Great damage was done mentally, emotionally and spiritually to his mentees and admirers. The cause of his fall was the fact that he trivialized the spirituality of his calling.

Donald recalled some of the statements of his pastor:
"If you do not learn from the fall of others, you are likely to be the next in line."
"You do not have to contact a killer disease in order to know its gravity or consequence."
"Those who refuse to learn from history will become victims of the same plights of their predecessors."

There were more than enough reasons why Donald had to make up his mind on handling his ministerial and secular life with all seriousness. In one of the regular sessions of his discussions with his mentor in the very early days of his encounter with the Lord, he had been tutored to learn from the lives of the fallen Christian generals. Being an ardent reader, he read about the life of Chuck Templeton, Bron Clifford and Billy Graham. The trios were "rivals" in ministry and friendship. In 1945, they were all rated as powerful speakers who turned the gospel world around. All three of these men with extraordinary gifts were actively involved in the service to the Lord. Within the space of ten years, two of them were out of the race.

BRON CLIFFORD:
He was a gifted young dynamic evangelist. He was sought after by many national leaders. He was very intelligent, handsome, sophisticated and dashing. In 1945, when he set out in the ministry, he was believed to be the most powerful preacher to come up in the

church for centuries. He won the endurance of people to line up to listen to him. His ministration at the famous Baylor University was off the chain. They actually cut the ropes off the bells of the tower so that his sermon will not be timed or interrupted. He was so captivating that he kept the students on edges of their seats as he gave a dissertation on "Christ and the Philosopher's Stone." At age 25, Clifford was credited with the achievement of touching more lives, influenced more leaders and set more attendance records than any other clergyman in American history.

By 1954, Clifford was addicted to alcohol. He lost his family and ministry to a vice that eventually wasted his life; alcoholism. He became financially reckless and irresponsible. He left his wife and two children who had Down's syndrome penniless. In his financial struggles, he became a trader of secondhand automobiles, a venture that was uneventful. He died of cirrhosis of the liver at the age of 35 in a rundown hotel on the edge of Amarillo, Texas, United States of America. He had nothing left of him to afford a befitting burial. Some pastors from Amarillo, Texas got some contributions to buy a cheap casket. He was buried in a pauper's cemetery.

CHARLES CHUCK TEMPLETON:

He was a handsome young man with amazing abilities and unlimited potentials. He was an early friend of Billy Graham [both in their twenties.] They both worked together in a very dynamic ministry called Youth For Christ. In 1946, the National Association of Evangelicals listed Templeton as the "best used of God. He had the largest Youth for Christ rally with over 2500 teens each Saturday night. Youth For Christ hired Billy Graham as evangelist-at-large on Chuck Templeton's recommendation. He was appointed to lead a team to Europe to promote Youth For Christ. Though he was a preacher of the gospel of Christ, he doubted the authenticity of many facts of the Bible, especially the story of creation and eternal hell fire for those who die in sin. In his efforts to overcome his doubts, he sought admission to a Bible college. His son said of him: "He went to the seminary to learn more and came out an agnostic." His secret doubt haunted him. He decided to end the whole charade and walked away from everything.

In his anecdotal memoir ["Age of Reason"] ability, he wrote: "I picked up Thomas Paine's "The Age of Reason. In a few hours, nearly everything I knew or believed about the Christian religion was challenged and in large part demolished." In the next ten days, he read Francois Voltaire's: 'The Bible Explained at Last'. Bertrand Russell's 'Why I am Not a Christian', the speeches of atheist, Robert Ingersoll, including 'The Mistakes of Moses', and some of the writings of David Hume and Thomas Huxley. At this juncture, Chuck was now doubting his beliefs and believing his doubts.

He left the ministry and drove with his family back to Canada where he began. He got cut off from all his friends and associates he had made in the ministry. He became unemployed with no prospect; he had stepped into the blackness of apostasy. He no longer believed in the God of the Bible.

He took a job as executive managing editor of the Toronto Star, Director of News for the Canadian Television Network and wrote twelve books. He wrote "Farewell to God" to justify his unbelief.

In an interview with him by Lee Strobel, a law graduate of Yale University who later became a legal editor for the Chicago Tribune who was once an atheist but become an advocate of the Christian faith shortly before he died. Strobel directed the aged Templeton's attention to Christ. He was asked how he would now assess Jesus at this stage of his life, he said: "He was the greatest human being who has ever lived. He was a moral genius. His ethical sense was unique. He was the intrinsically wisest person that I've ever encountered in my life or in my reading. His commitment was total and led to his own death, much to the detriment of the world."

Strobel quietly commented: "You sound like you really care about him." "Well, yes," Templeton acknowledged, "he's the most important thing in my life." He stammered: "I...I...I adore him...Everything good I know, everything decent I know, everything pure I know, I learned from Jesus." His voice began to crack, he then said, "I miss... him!"

Charles Templeton's final days were spent in decline due to Alzheimer's [A progressive mental deterioration]. He passed from this life on June 7, 2001 at the age of 85.
[Adapted from Christian courier... internet articles >328-sk. A skeptic reflect on Jesus Christ]]

BILLY GRAHAM
William Franklin Graham Jr was born on November 7, 1918, in the downstairs bedroom of a farmhouse near Charlotte, North Carolina. He was of Scots-Irish descent. He was raised by his parents in the Associate Reformed Presbyterian Church. Graham was 16 years old in 1934 when he was converted during a series of revival meetings that Ham led in Charlotte.

In 1937, Graham transferred to the Florida Bible Institute in Temple Terrace, Florida. He preached his first sermon that year at Bostwick Baptist Church near Palatka, Florida while still a student. In his autobiography, Graham wrote that he received his "calling on the 18th green of the Temple Terrace Golf and Country Club"

In 1943-1944, Graham briefly served as the pastor of the First Baptist Church in Western Springs, Illinois. In 1945, all three of these men [Charles Chuck Templeton, Bron Clifford, and Billy Graham] with extraordinary gifts were actively involved in the service to the Lord. Within the space of ten years two out of the three were no more in the ministry.

Graham was 29 years old in 1948 when he became president of Northwestern Bible College in Minneapolis. He was the youngest president of a college or university in the country and held the position for four years before he resigned in 1952. He was hired as the first full-time evangelist of the new "Youth for Christ" [YFC], co-founded by Torrey Johnson and the Canadian evangelist, Charles Templeton.

Graham spoke at the InterVersity Christian Fellowship's Urbana Students Missions Conference at least nine times- in 1948,1957, 1961, 1964, 1976, 1979, 1981, 1984 and 1987. At each Urbana conference, he challenged the thousands of attendees to make a commitment to follow Jesus Christ for the rest of their lives. He often quoted a six-word phrase that was reportedly written in the Bible of William Whiting Borden, "No reserves, no retreat, and no regret."

In 1950, Graham founded the Billy Graham Evangelistic Association [BGEA] with its headquarters in Minneapolis. The association relocated to Charlotte, North Carolina in 1999.

Apart from being a preacher, he was a salient Civil Rights protagonist. His early crusades were segregated but he began adjusting his approach in the 1950s. During a 1953 rally in Chattanooga, Tennessee, Graham tore down the ropes that organizers had erected in order to segregate the audience to racial sections. He warned a white audience, "We have been proud and thought we were better than any other race, any other people. Ladies and gentlemen, we are going to stumble into hell because of our pride."
In 1957, he allowed black ministers Thomas Kilgore and Gardner C. Taylor to serve as members of his New York Crusade's executive committee and invited the Rev. Martin Luther King Jr whom he first met during the Montgomery bus boycott in 1955 to join him in the pulpit at his 16-week revival in New York City, where 2.3 million gathered. He was of the opinion that "There is no scriptural base for segregation."

Billy Graham died February 21, 2018 in Montreal, NC. USA. *[Adapted from Wikipedia.]*

EVANGELIST ASA ALONSO ALLEN

A. A. Allen was born March 27, 1911 In Sulphur Rock Arkansas USA. He died June 11, 1970 in San Francisco, California USA.

He was a renowned healing evangelist. A lot of controversies pervaded his life. He was purportedly reported to have died an alcoholic at the age of 59.

Donald was overwhelmed by his findings about many notable ministers who had evident callings from the Lord but ended badly. He could not get over Apostle Paul's admonition: "Therefore let the one who thinks he stands firm [immune to temptation, being overconfident and self-righteous], take care that he does not fall [into sin and condemnation]. No temptation [regardless of its source] has overtaken or enticed you that is not common to human experience [nor is any temptation unusual or beyond human resistance]; but God is faithful [to His word—He is compassionate and trustworthy], and He will not let you be tempted beyond your ability [to resist], but along with the temptation He [has in the past and is now and] will [always] provide the way out as well, so that you will be able to endure it [without yielding, and will overcome temptation with joy]."
1Corinthians 10:12-13 AMP

"We do not have the audacity to put ourselves in the same class or compare ourselves with some who

[supply testimonials to] commend themselves. When they measure themselves by themselves and compare themselves with themselves, they lack wisdom and behave like fools. We, on the other hand, will not boast beyond our proper limit, but [will keep] within the limits of our commission (territory, authority) which God has granted to us as a measure, which reaches and includes even you."
2 Corinthians 10:12-13 AMP

"Inasmuch then as we [believers] have a great High Priest who has [already ascended and] passed through the heavens, Jesus the Son of God, let us hold fast our confession [of faith and cling tenaciously to our absolute trust in Him as Savior]. For we do not have a High Priest who is unable to sympathize and understand our weaknesses and temptations, but One who has been tempted [knowing exactly how it feels to be human] in every respect as we are, yet without [committing any] sin." Hebrews 4:14-15 AMP

The statement of his pastor: "Lucifer and his cohorts are no fools; they do not make cheap choices," kept ringing in his subconscious.

He conclusively asserted:
"When it comes to the issues of calling in the Christian ministry, it is not how any individual started that is of much importance or significance but how he or she finishes the race."

CHAPTER FIVE

THE RACE

Race is a competition between runners. The ministerial calling is the second leg of the Christian race; the race is not a sprint but a marathon. Not many finishes well or get to the finishing line before they were finished by the enemy of their soul. The devil had been a good runner and a terrible "Roam-about," as recorded in the scriptures:

"The LORD said to Satan, "From where have you come?" Then Satan answered the LORD, "From roaming around on the earth and from walking around on it." Job 1:7 AMP

He knows his rights and learns compliance when he gets a divinely endorsed resistance.

The Bible says:

"So submit to [the authority of] God. Resist the devil [stand firm against him] and he will flee from you."
James 4:7 AMP

He has the ability to flee where need be. To flee is a more propitious action for safety. A true submission on the part of a Christian to the Lord makes the individual holy and empowered for survival in the race of life and ministry.

Donald had always been a determined Christian. He did not take any situation as a game of chance. His formal approach on issues is subject to the dictates of the spirit in line with the scriptures.

He relished the scripture:
"Rejoice always and delight in your faith; be unceasing and persistent in prayer; in every situation [no matter what the circumstances] be thankful and continually give thanks to God; for this is the will of God for you in Christ Jesus. Do not quench [subdue, or be unresponsive to the working and guidance of] the [Holy] Spirit. Do not scorn or reject gifts of prophecy or prophecies [spoken revelations—words of instruction or exhortation or warning]. But test all things carefully [so you can recognize what is good]. Hold firmly to that which is good. Abstain from every form of evil [withdraw and keep away from it]. Now may the God of peace Himself sanctify you through and through [that is, separate you from profane and vulgar things, make you pure and whole and undamaged—consecrated to Him—set apart for His purpose]; and may your spirit and soul and body be kept complete and [be found] blameless at the coming of our Lord Jesus Christ. Faithful and absolutely trustworthy is He who is calling you [to Himself for

your salvation], and He will do it [He will fulfill His call by making you holy, guarding you, watching over you, and protecting you as His own]."
1 Thessalonians 5:16-24 AMP

He learnt a lot from one of the sermons of his pastor, titled: "THE FAITHFUL RUNNER." His pastor laid emphasis on the differences between the "faithful runner" and the "able runner." According to him, the able and the faithful may run together. The faithful is always guided by the rule of the game. The able may not pay attention to the rules. He inferred that God does not need human ability but availability and readiness to comply with divine instruction. He referred to the statement of Apostle Paul:

"Do you not know that in a race all the runners run [their very best to win], but only one receives the prize? Run [your race] in such a way that you may seize the prize and make it yours! Now every athlete who [goes into training and] competes in the games is disciplined and exercises self-control in all things. They do it to win a crown that withers, but we [do it to receive] an imperishable [crown that cannot wither]. Therefore I do not run without a definite goal; I do not flail around like one beating the air [just shadow boxing]. But [like a boxer] I strictly discipline my body and make it my slave, so that, after I have preached [the gospel] to others, I myself will not somehow be disqualified [as unfit for service]."
1 Corinthians 9:24-27 AMP

He believed every runner should always ask for the mercies of God in the course of the race. He said: "In the contemporary athletic competition, the best runner may pull a muscle almost at the finishing line. He told his listeners not to lose sight of the assertion of Apostle Paul:

"For He says to Moses, "I WILL HAVE MERCY ON WHOMEVER I HAVE MERCY, AND I WILL HAVE COMPASSION ON WHOMEVER I HAVE COMPASSION." So then God's choice is not dependent on human will, nor on human effort [the totality of human striving], but on God who shows mercy [to whomever He chooses—it is His sovereign gift]." Rom. 9:15-16 AMP

He however cautioned: "This does not mean that God endorsed indolence, laziness or nonperformance."

Conclusively, he said: "If you value your destination, you will keep the rules of the race and journey. Always remember that we are going beyond this world. Apostle Paul wrote:

"If we who are [abiding] in Christ have hoped only in this life [and this is all there is], then we are of all people most miserable and to be pitied."
1 Corinthians 15:19 AMP.

Donald was lost in thought when Pastor Henry, his senior pastor-friend, walked in. Though there were marginal age and hierarchical gap between them, they still related as friends due to the sobriety, humility and spiritual enthusiasm of Donald. A tap on his shoulder called his attention. He was questioned: "What were you thinking about?" With a great sigh, he said: "Sir, I do not know where to start. It's all about this Christian race. Sir, did you hear about the death of Pastor Niyod?" "O yes, that was very disturbing!" responded Pastor Henry. "Is it true that he committed suicide?" "I guess not, but rumor has it so." "Well, we are not in any position to confirm or deny the assumptions. The fact remains that he has ended the race." Pastor Henry took a deep breath and said; "I wish he knew the spirituality of his calling." "How do you mean?" responded Donald. "I heard so much about the controversies that surrounded his life as a pastor. Many had negative impression of him but probably were not bold enough to confront him, or counsel him." "You know he was a highly placed minister of the gospel, and had very few people who could call him to order. Even if they attempted to, he may not listen to them. One of his colleagues told me he spoke with him at the assumed beginning of his derangement and defiance but he would not listen." "I guess the key reason responsible for his adamance was the success of his ministry," Donald asserted. "There is no doubt, his conscience was seared with hot iron as Apostle Paul stated" responded Pastor Henry.

"But the [Holy] Spirit explicitly and unmistakably declares that in later times some will turn away from the faith, paying attention instead to deceitful and seductive spirits and doctrines of demons, [misled] by the hypocrisy of liars whose consciences are seared as with a branding iron [leaving them incapable of ethical functioning]." 1 Timothy 4:1-2 AMP

Pastor Henry was hesitant to talk more about the lifestyle of Pastor Niyod. Looking at Donald, with an air of despondency, he said: "Would you believe that I have had to investigate this same pastor for over a decade?" Sir, what about?" "Similar or related issue of course!" "Why were we not informed long before it became a popular and controversial rumor? Sir, you know he was our guest speaker at many of our programs!" "Well, it would not be ministerally ethical to indict him for an unauthenticated allegation. He was a very intelligent and crafty character. He played safe in most instances. The fact however remains that no one can outwit God."

With his hand supporting his chin in a recline of his head, Donald groaned: "Over a decade? God had been very merciful to him. I guess he got familiar with God. Did he understand the implication of his illicit relationships? Though I heard that his wife was greatly emotionally disturbed, stressed and distressed. I learnt she did everything possible to protect the image of her husband. But I never believed there was any truth in the rumor." "You may need to realize that in any rumor, there may always be an element of truth, though it may be distorted. It is very important that a minister of the gospel of Jesus Christ creates no room for suspicion or rumor around his or her life." Henry interrupted. Donald went on: "Sir, in your capacity as a senior pastor and investigator, why didn't you recommend his suspension based on the controversies?" With a tincture of enigmatic smile, he retorted: "Suspicion on sex related issues will generate heat and clamor that may dent the image of the officer who raised the red flag."

With a smile, Pastor Henry said: "I guess you may learn something from this true life story of an incident that happened when I was a teenager."
"That must be many years ago," Donald laughingly interrupted;
He went on; "We lived in a compound with families and relatives. Some of the occupants were tenants of my father. On one occasion a cousin of mine was purportedly caught in an illicit sexual relationship with one of the daughters of a tenant. He was in full blast when the younger sister of his partner walked into the room. She screamed at them and later reported the incident to her mother, Mrs. Brooks. She was very angry and ferocious as she yelled through the compound.

Mrs. Brooks went straight, accusing my cousin of violation of her teenage daughter. My cousin denied any sexual involvement with her daughter. She brought her daughter forward with some rough handlings before everybody. Her daughter denied ever getting involved in any act of sex with my cousin.

Jenny who saw them in the act was viewed as stupid and out of her mind. She cried and wept bitterly without the ability to convince everyone that she was in her right mind. From that moment, I made up my mind to be very careful on issues of sexual allegations.

It was a sober moment for them both. Pastor Henry with a stern look and a vexation in his spirit, said: "It is strange that many whom one would think would be reasonable enough to appreciate the mercies of God shown to Pastor Niyod were very emotional and sentimental on the issue. They viewed his death as a blow that cast aspersion on the image of the church. In reality, they should have seen his death as a cleansing of the church. If such had happened in the days of old, he would have died in the "Holy of Holies." He asserted.

"Sir, I guess most of the Christians of our days do not see God as a Consuming Fire or Lion of the tribe of Judah. He is said to be the God of mercy and Jesus as the Lamb of God." "That is not the absolute truth. The fact is that they are not conscious of the position and presence of Lucifer in the race for eternity in heaven. If they are, they will not trivialize issues that affect both physical and eternal experience," Pastor Henry submitted.

Donald, with a gesture of respect and apology, said:
"Sir, as you were talking, I just realized the
implication of Apostle Paul's letter to the Hebrews":
"Therefore, since we are surrounded by so great a
cloud of witnesses [who by faith have testified to the
truth of God's absolute faithfulness], stripping off
every unnecessary weight and the sin which so easily
and cleverly entangles us, let us run with endurance
and active persistence the race that is set before us,
[looking away from all that will distract us and]
focusing our eyes on Jesus, who is the Author and
Perfecter of faith [the first incentive for our belief and
the One who brings our faith to maturity], who for the
joy [of accomplishing the goal] set before Him
endured the cross, disregarding the shame, and sat
down at the right hand of the throne of God [revealing
His deity, His authority, and the completion of His
work]." Hebrews 12:1-2 AMP

"I do not mean to drag you into theological argument
or analysis; please do not be too assertive about the
author of the book of Hebrews. The very author is not
known. I do agree with you that it looks like the style
of writing of Apostle Paul but for the omission of his
traditional opening statement, "Paul an Apostle..."
Pastor Henry cautioned. "Sir, you are right, on that
note. I am just too much in love with Apostle Paul. I
may not agree with his self-exalting statement that he
labored more than other disciples or apostles". With a

broad smile Pastor Henry affirmed that, that was the reason the Lord decided to tame him with an infirmity that compelled his total submission to God and respect for others. As stated in his second letter to the Corinthian brethren:

"Because of the surpassing greatness and extraordinary nature of the revelations [which I received from God], for this reason, to keep me from thinking of myself as important, a thorn in the flesh was given to me, a messenger of Satan, to torment and harass me—to keep me from exalting myself! Concerning this I pleaded with the Lord three times that it might leave me; but He has said to me, "My grace is sufficient for you [My loving-kindness and My mercy are more than enough—always available—regardless of the situation]; for [My] power is being perfected [and is completed and shows itself most effectively] in [your] weakness." Therefore, I will all the more gladly boast in my weaknesses, so that the power of Christ [may completely enfold me and] may dwell in me. So I am well pleased with weaknesses, with insults, with distresses, with persecutions, and with difficulties, for the sake of Christ; for when I am weak [in human strength], then I am strong [truly able, truly powerful, truly drawing from God's strength]. Now I have become foolish; you have forced me [by questioning my apostleship]. Actually I should have been commended by you [instead of being treated

disdainfully], for I was not inferior to those super-apostles, even if I am nobody."
2 Corinthians 12:7-11 AMP

Donald was reluctant to talk any further, but said; "I wish the Lord had tamed Pastor Niyod long before his eventual destruction." With a deep sigh, Pastor Henry responded: "I am very sure the Lord must have spoken to him, cautioned him or warned him through the power of the spoken or written word. He must have been recalcitrant. Remember that the Bible says, "He who hardens his neck and refuses instruction after being often reproved (corrected, criticized), Will suddenly be broken beyond repair." Prov. 29:1 AMP

It was time for them to part. Pastor Henry was very valedictory in his closing remarks. He said: "My beloved Pastor Donald..." He was spontaneously interrupted by Donald in attempt to correct the designation or conferment of the title "Pastor" on him. In refutation he said: "Sir, I am not a pastor but a deacon." "I guess my pronouncement is a prophetic utterance. You will surely be conferred with the ordination as a pastor during the coming convention." Pastor Henry unequivocally assured.

"Back to my admonition before your interruption, well, I guess the Lord made you interrupt me to confirm His plan for you in the ministry. You should realize that the Christian race is pervaded with diverse challenges. Your Area Pastor had already informed me about your reluctance to accept the pastoral responsibility. That is typical of the true materials for spiritual leadership. Remember the statement of the author of the letter to the Hebrews: "And besides, one does not appropriate for himself the honor [of being high priest], but he who is called by God, just as Aaron was. So too Christ did not glorify Himself so as to be made a high priest, but He [was exalted and appointed by the One] who said to Him, "YOU ARE MY SON, TODAY I HAVE BEGOTTEN (fathered) YOU [declared Your authority and rule over the nations]" Hebrews 5:4-5 AMP

My prayer is that the Lord will uphold you and strengthen the good work He has been doing through you and in your life. I pray He will guide you perfectly on the ground of marital relationship.

Donald could not resist a shout of "AMEN" when Pastor Henry [his District Pastor] mentioned the issue of his matrimonial settlement. He continued with his admonition: "Marriage could be a great determinant of attainment or accomplishment of any individual in this Christian race. May I caution you not to marry any lady on the basis of her beauty but her spirituality and commitment to the things of the Lord. Remember the biblical counseling of the mother of King Solomon in the book of Proverbs 31. The 30th verse is very crucial. It states:

"Charm and grace are deceptive, and [superficial] beauty is vain, But a woman who fears the LORD [reverently worshiping, obeying, serving, and trusting Him with awe-filled respect], she shall be praised." Proverbs 31:30 AMP.

I am praying for you and will be ready to do my best to see to it that you are better than me in the ministry. Since the day I met with you I have determined to see you excel. I strongly believe that the greatest frustration of any successful leader so as it were would be the inability to produce a better successor. May the Lord keep you and perfect all that concerns you. May you not disappoint God. May you not disappoint those of us that appreciate Christ in your life. May you not disappoint yourself." Donald shouted a very resounding AMEN!

Right in the presence of Donald, Pastor Henry called his wife to notify her of his current location and the other places he would likely get to before his return home. He apologized for staying a little longer than expected. He explained that he had been with Deacon Donald. He handed him the phone hand-set for him to say hello to his wife. Donald apologized to Pastor [Mrs.] Henry for keeping him a little longer than planned. She responded: "I am neither surprised nor offended, that is always the case when a son is a friend of the father." With a broad smile and a mild laughter, he thanked her for her understanding and love. Pastor Henry walked towards his car, waved to Donald and prayed: "...May the Lord continue to give you the grace to remain faithful to the end in the race. It was a good parting.

Donald was still in the shock of the privileged information of his proposed ordination as a pastor in the next few months. He had never seen himself as a material good enough to be a pastor. He was not sure what his married life was going to look like. He was taken aback when he remembered the plight of one of the pastors in the nearby city whose ministry had nose-dived due to the crises in his matrimony. He felt he was at a cross-road in the race. He determined to pray fervently and solicit the prayer support of his trusted friends in the ministry. He remembered one of the statements of his Area Pastor that mentored him and launched him into the ministry.

"If you want to last in the race, make sure your steps can be traced."
In his rumination, he remembered one of the brethren that answered the alter call the same day with him who had backslidden. He was not able to advance any possible reason that could have led to his departure from the faith. He could only recall an occasion when the brother was sharply reprimanded for wrong comportment. To him, that would not be a strong enough reason for someone to deny or renounce the lordship of Jesus Christ. He could not imagine how

easy it could be for a promising Christian to be easily knocked out of the race by the devil.

Flipping through his Bible he opened and read:
"I again saw under the sun that the race is not to the swift and the battle is not to the strong, and neither is bread to the wise nor riches to those of intelligence and understanding nor favor to men of ability; but time and chance overtake them all. For man also does not know his time [of death]; like fish caught in a treacherous net, and birds caught in the snare, so the sons of men are ensnared in an evil time when a dark cloud suddenly falls on them."
Ecclesiastes 9:11-12 AMP

He meditated on these verses of the scripture. He felt he could almost hear an audible voice expounding the scripture to his understanding. The two words that struck strong chords in his mind were "time" and "chance". He had been told; "Time is money." He heard in his spirit that time is much more than money. "Time is life." He thought about what he could do to maximize his time to cover more ground in the race. He realized that good use of time is a factor that increases the chances of any individual's success. He had heard a preacher say: "He who wastes your time wastes your life." He concluded that time is the life of the race. His understanding of the 12th verse was deepened by the power of the Spirit. "*So the sons of men are ensnared in an evil time when a dark cloud suddenly falls on them."* He was informed that man may have to be chased by the snare or walk into the snare according to the lustful desire of the individual. Man may be led into temptation or walk into temptation. He realized that man could only be ensnared when the darkness of sin takes over the life of the individual at a moment referred to as an evil time.

With every sense of seriousness he ruminated upon:
"Let no one say when he is tempted, "I am being tempted by God" [for temptation does not originate from God, but from our own flaws]; for God cannot be tempted by [what is] evil, and He Himself tempts no one. But each one is tempted when he is dragged away, enticed and baited [to commit sin] by his own [worldly] desire (lust, passion). Then when the illicit desire has conceived, it gives birth to sin; and when sin has run its course, it gives birth to death."
James 1:13-15 AMP

He found solace in the letter of Apostle Paul to the brethren in Philippi:
"Finally, believers, whatever is true, whatever is honorable and worthy of respect, whatever is right and confirmed by God's word, whatever is pure and wholesome, whatever is lovely and brings peace, whatever is admirable and of good repute; if there is any excellence, if there is anything worthy of praise,

think continually on these things [center your mind on them, and implant them in your heart]. The things which you have learned and received and heard and seen in me, practice these things [in daily life], and the God [who is the source] of peace and well-being will be with you." Philippians 4:8-9 AMP

In his personal conclusions, he agreed that anyone that would finish well in the Christian race must have self-discipline and never engage in any pity-party in the course of the journey on the rough road to heaven. The race is not a sprint but a marathon.

==
"Marriage could be a great determinant
of attainment or accomplishment of any
individual in this Christian race
==

CHAPTER SIX

LIFE! A MARATHON

It is never the desire of anyone to make life or any pleasant experience a "sprint". Life as designed by God is expected to be a marathon. A marathon is a long-lasting race, a difficult or challenging task. Many "marathons" may come in disguise. There are many instances that man may assume would be "sprint" that may end up being "marathons." Because life is designed to be a marathon, man is mandatorily billed to pass through diverse moments; pleasant and challenging moments alike.

The perception of circumstances of life by various individuals determines the response of the person to the experience. Reaction to experience is determined by the force or spirit that is in control of the individual.

The Bible states: "Now to Him who is able to [carry out His purpose and] do superabundantly more than all that we dare ask or think [infinitely beyond our greatest prayers, hopes, or dreams], according to His power that is at work within us,"Ephesians 3:20 AMP

Life is a race, the individual's consciousness and sensitivity to the desired accomplishments or destination determines the adherence to and compliance with the rules of the journey. Noncompliance with guiding rules or principles is the greatest bait that could lead to losses and non-accomplishment of the desired goal.

Many "lives", physical, matrimonial, ministerial, spiritual... had been cut short [turned into "sprint" instead of "marathon"] due to carelessness, non-chalance, negative idiosyncrasies, negligence and ignorance of the spirituality of calling or purpose. In some cases, it had been better or would have been better that some "marathons" were reduced to "sprint" to save the face of the affected. There were many biblical characters or instances that epitomized this assertion.

Donald, in his quest for safety through the knowledge of the word of God, made good studies of some characters in the Bible.

KING DAVID
Many that were called by God from obscurity into prominence very soon fell victims of the deceitfulness of comfort. Comfort can make man forget past struggles and hardship. Comfort is a springboard to trivialities, negligence and infatuations that could lead

to undue indulgences. However comfort is the desire and aspiration of almost everybody.

King David was one of such characters in the scripture who suffered relegation before he was accorded divine recognition and elevation, which granted him popularity and acceptance by humanity. He was a shepherd-boy made king. If kingship was to be determined by election, he would not have won the primaries even in his own family ward. [1Samuel 16: 1-13.]

On the day of his divine recognition and elevation, he was nowhere to be found around the location of his promotion from relegation to divine ordination and kingly consecration. They had to look for him.
The Bible states:

"Then Samuel said to Jesse, "Are all your sons here?" Jesse replied, "There is still one left, the youngest; he is tending the sheep." Samuel said to Jesse, "Send word and bring him; because we will not sit down [to eat the sacrificial meal] until he comes here. So Jesse sent word and brought him in. Now he had a ruddy complexion, with beautiful eyes and a handsome appearance. The LORD said [to Samuel], "Arise, anoint him; for this is he." Then Samuel took the horn of oil and anointed David in the presence of his brothers; and the Spirit of the LORD came mightily upon David from that day forward. And Samuel arose and went to Ramah." 1 Samuel 16:11-13 AMP.

The journey of the life of David to the throne of Israel was not a sprint. He passed through a lot of challenging moments.

He had to play music for "mad King Saul", though he was himself anointed to be king.

He fought and killed Goliath of Gath.

He narrowly escaped the javelins of King Saul.

He ran from pillar to post trying to escape death in the hands of King Saul.

He was a victim of suppression and oppression in the hands of Abner, the then captain of the army of Israel under King Ishboshet, the son of King Saul.

He waited seven years after the death of King Saul, before he became king over the whole of Israel.

One would easily have assumed that the rough road to the throne would have tamed the lust of his flesh.

He soon got into comfort and affluence of sovereignty and forgot the days of his challenges. He very soon forgot the purpose for which the Lord put him in the position of king over the land of Israel. He forgot the spirituality of his calling.

Self-discipline is the secret to survival in the "marathons" of life. Those who understand the spirituality of their calling do not indulge themselves. Indulgence is not a mark of love but a bait of destruction.

Self-discipline demands that one does the right thing at the right time.

Be at the right place at the right time.

Do the right thing every day, not because of every day but because of one day. Consistency in doing the right thing averts the evils of the doom-day.

Jesus said:

"But first and most importantly seek (aim at, strive after) His kingdom and His righteousness [His way of doing and being right—the attitude and character of God], and all these things will be given to you also. "So do not worry about tomorrow; for tomorrow will worry about itself. Each day has enough trouble of its own." Matthew 6:33-34 AMP

A good understanding of the spirituality of calling demands sobriety and compliance with rules and regulations put in place for the accomplishment of purpose. King David soon forgot that battles keep a good soldier on his or her toes. He was not occupied by the things of the kingdom upon which he was made a king. He was preoccupied with the dictates of comfort. He did not realize that there is no vacuum in nature. "You either occupy or be occupied." "Wrong occupation is the bane of catastrophe. " He sent his subordinate officers to the battle field while he remained in the enclave of comfort. **There is no doubt that the devil finds work for the idle hand. Any soldier that desires to finish well in the marathon of life must be fully occupied. Good occupation is a safety valve.**

The Bible states:

"Then it happened in the spring, at the time when the kings go out to battle, that David sent Joab and his servants with him, and all [the fighting men of] Israel, and they destroyed the Ammonites and besieged Rabbah. But David remained in Jerusalem. One evening David got up from his couch and was walking on the [flat] roof of the king's palace, and from there he saw a woman bathing; and she was very beautiful in appearance."2 Samuel 11:1-2 AMP

The greatest dent in the armor of King David was not sustained when he fought against Goliath but it stemmed from his self-indulgence and noncompliance with the principles that sustained his position as a leader. He trivialized the spirituality of his calling.

He messed up big time with Bathsheba and thus exposed himself to a near death encounter with God. His attempt to cover up his atrocity of sexual promiscuity led to the murder of Uriah, a valiant and faithful soldier. It was a major curse and the beginning of his challenges as a king over the nation of Israel.

As long as life persists, human experience is a "marathon". The nature of the experience will be determined by the individual's values and ambition. The experience of King David would have drifted him away from God. However, his personal desire to please God brought him into repentance which eventually qualified him to be called a friend of God. It is not the height of an individual's righteousness that endears him or her to God but the individual's brokenness and readiness to please God. Sanctification is a necessity that births righteousness in the sight of God. Human righteousness is like filthy rags compared with the holiness of God. [Isaiah 64: 6]. However, holiness is required to approach the presence of God. Those who understand the spirituality of their callings do not play game with God.

THE MAN: JOSEPH

Joseph was a man with intrinsic righteousness. There was no mention of his receiving tutorials on moral uprightness or piety. His life was however an epitome of righteousness and Godliness. He had no clear understanding of his dreams; his life experience negated his aspirations. The people he worked hard to please turn out to be his enemies and forces of opposition that sold him into slavery. He nurtured his aspiration on the principles of holiness as evident in his comportment in the house of his slave master, Potiphar. He understood that sexual promiscuity is a sin against God. He was a righteous man of no compromise. His holiness landed him into the Egyptian jail. His piety and empathy granted him favor in the sight of the chief warden. He lived as someone who had adequate knowledge of the spirituality of his calling. There was no record of impropriety or sins that can be appropriated to the person of Joseph.

Every would-be successful minister of the gospel of Jesus needs to pay attention to the life of Joseph. He had no title or position to protect but the image of God whom he personally chose to represent. He was a self-made ambassador of the Most High God. He was a divinely prepared vessel justified by providence to fulfill divine mandate. His personal comportment was the cream of his personality which eventually made him a darling of his acquaintances.

He had a burning desire for freedom but would not wangle his way through undue liberty. He pleaded for remembrance but was forgotten until God's appointed time. On the day of his appointment with destiny, he was not clean enough to stand in the presence of Pharaoh; not because of his personal filth but the mark of the prison and branding as a prisoner. His inner purity for thirteen years paid off. It had fought relentlessly against his outward filth to grant him a change of garment and brought him to the presence of Pharaoh the king of Egypt.

The inherent nature of the omniscience of God paved way for him in the presence of Pharaoh and afforded him access to the seat as the first Prime Minister of Egypt. He saved the entire then known world from starvation for the preservation of humanity. Hunger brought his adversaries and rival siblings to bow before him as revealed to his ignorance many years back. His magnanimity preserved the lives of his siblings who were the evil chariots that brought him into Egypt in the first place. He had no room for bitterness. He eschewed un-forgiveness but relished divine insight, that he was sent ahead of his siblings to preserve the entire family. He knew all things were to work for the good of those who served and obeyed God in holiness and absolute purity. Obviously everything worked for his good to fulfill divine mandate. His mother was the only one who did not live long enough to fulfill her side of obeisance as revealed in his dream.

Donald viewed Joseph as a man with immaculate character, a standard he desired to attain. In his imaginations, he wished everyone involved in the Christian ministry would imbibe in the character and determined purity of Joseph. He bowed his head and prayed:

"O Lord, thank you for the salvation of my soul.

I thank you for how far you have helped me in my short walk with you.

I pray my walk with you is a marathon that will usher me into heaven.

Father, have mercy on me. Give me the grace to forgive my adversaries.

I am yet to acquire the spiritual maturity of Joseph.

O Lord, grant me the wisdom and revelation knowledge to see beyond the ordinary.
Father, deliver me from vain imaginations. Keep me focused on you.
My Father and my Lord, please cleanse me of all inner filth.
Lord Jesus, please grant me a change of raiment.
By your grace O Lord, preserve me to preserve lives.
Have mercy on me and count me worthy to spend eternity with you in heaven."

He opened his eyes only to realize that a strange figure was present with him in the room. He could not clearly discern the nature and motive of the appearance of the figure. He had a mental imagery of the figure as an angel of the Lord. How he concluded, he could not explain. He had a ministration in his spirit that he was being empowered to fulfill his purpose in the pastoral ministry. The vision, illusion or hallucination was done with. He wiped his face with the palm of his hands as someone emerging or recovering from a trance. He knew he had a divine encounter but could not even explain to his personal reasoning for any clear understanding. He felt excited in his spirit and determined to live a life of purity and holiness.

The experience of what he could only describe as a trance prompted his inquisitions into the operations and ministries of angels. He concluded that angels do not necessarily have wings. He realized that the life of Joseph had impacted his spirit beyond his wildest imagination. He determined to have further discussions with his mentors on the subject. With a radiant smile across his face he said: "There is no end to seeking knowledge of the word of God. Ministry is a marathon nourished and nurtured by good knowledge of the word of God."

There was someone at the door, Donald soliloquized: "I wish it is the angel that I saw few minutes ago. It was Jeremiah, one of his converts. In his thoughts, he desired to be "fed," he was not ready to "breast-feed." His thoughts were evident in his response to the presence of his uninvited guest. He had the least impression that he was detestable and obviously repugnant to the presence of his convert. "I am sorry to disturb you. I am just anxious to share with you something I read in this book; Donald Oren —- "ANGELS ON ASSIGNMENTS", about the ministry of angels. I guess you are very busy right now. I will surely be ready to come back any time you will be available to listen to me. I am sure you must have read about angels over the years."

Donald was very eager to listen to Jeremiah; he regretted his attitude which he never meant to make known to his convert. He tendered an unreserved apology. He said: "Bro. Jerry, please forgive my hostility. I just had a disturbing, yet exciting experience that made me desire to meet one of my mentors for better enlightenment about the ministry of angels. I guess you are the prepared vessel the Lord had planned to bring me the information. I guess you are my angel. Jeremiah smiled to reciprocate the radiance of Donald. The atmosphere changed. He took the book from him and called his attention to the coincidence of the name of the author. They both laughed. "God has a good sense of humor," asserted Jeremiah.

It was a nice time as Jeremiah gave a summary of the averagely voluminous book. With a sense of humor, he said: "...I don't have to sleep here trying to share the content of the entire book with you, neither am I prepared to leave the book behind." He opened to one of the pages. They carefully read about how angels may reveal the mind of God to man. After a good sharing of pleasantries, Donald turned to Jeremiah and said: "You are an angel." Jeremiah stretched out his arms as if he was about to fly. "You have just convinced me that angels do not necessarily have wings. Are you trying to deny being one or trying to convince me that you are one of the cherubs?" They both laughed. The aspect that; "angels have the ability to take on human nature" was the most interesting part of the abilities of the angels. The conclusion was that any human being can be "an angel" when under the influence of the spirit of God to enforce the extra ordinary.

Donald ruminated upon the statement of Apostle Paul to the Philippians:

"And this, so that I may know Him [experientially, becoming more thoroughly acquainted with Him, understanding the remarkable wonders of His Person more completely] and [in that same way experience] the power of His resurrection [which overflows and is active in believers], and [that I may share] the fellowship of His sufferings, by being continually conformed [inwardly into His likeness even] to His death [dying as He did];" Philippians 3:10 AMP

He could not imagine or get over the fact that Jeremiah was the one God chose to minister to him at such a crucial moment of his life. He soliloquized; "I guess I am yet to know or probably I am getting to know God. Learning is actually a marathon." He remembered his pastor saying: "Learning is a spring of inspiration, to fail to learn is to learn to fail. Learning saves life."

Jeremiah departed with a sense of fulfillment, meeting the need of his mentor. Donald was impressed that his convert was desirous to know more about the faith than just the basics to which he was introduced. He was excited when he remembered that he spoke to Jeremiah and other converts about the Berean Christians. The Bible says:

"The brothers immediately sent Paul and Silas away by night to Berea; and when they arrived, they entered the Jewish synagogue. Now these people were more noble and open-minded than those in Thessalonica, so they received the message [of salvation through faith in the Christ] with great eagerness, examining the Scriptures daily to see if these things were so. As a result many of them became believers, together with a number of prominent Greek women and men."
Acts 17:10-12 AMP

He conclusively asserted that, "Nobility in Christianity is attained by personal knowledge of the Lord through the scriptures and the inspiration of the Holy Spirit." He realized that most of his converts had learnt from him; the importance of good study of the scriptures and Christian books.

The thought, "If life is a marathon, challenges will not cease in the acquisition of knowledge. Experience is not sold in the market; it is in reality acquired at the cost of mistakes. Whatever man passes through, as long as it does not cost life, becomes part of his or her experience."

He remembered the statement of late Pastor Miles Monroe: "The wealthiest place on the planet is just down the road. It is the cemetery. There lie buried companies that were never started, inventions that were never made, bestselling books that were never written, and masterpieces that were never painted. In the cemetery is buried the greatest treasure of untapped potentials" He determined to make the best of time and opportunities. He was restless about mobilizing his converts and members of his local congregation to make the best of the gifts of God in their lives. In his opinion, he was bent on impacting his converts and members spiritually and materially. He believed that the church should be a place of adequate information for the betterment of the lives of Christians. Though he believed that the church is the ground to prepare Christians for heaven; he had an opinion that no one should be too heaven conscious and earthly irrelevant.

In his studies of the lives of many Christians of old, he realized that Christianity is not just a call to pleasure and aspiration for the treasures of heaven. It has always been a call unto challenges and determination to make a difference in a world that is pervaded and perverted by sin. As young, unmarried minister of the gospel, he developed a personal hatred for the sexual innuendos associated with advertisement and publications across the world. He hated pornography. However he realized that it was a struggle and challenging task avoiding it on the social media. He purposed just like Daniel did in the scripture that he would not defile himself with the king's meal... Daniel 1: 8.

He took his Bible and read:

"I have made a covenant (agreement) with my eyes; how then could I gaze [lustfully] at a virgin? For what is the portion I would have from God above, and what heritage from the Almighty on high? Does not tragedy fall [justly] on the unjust And disaster to those who work wickedness? Does not God see my ways And count all my steps? "If I have walked with falsehood, Or if my foot has chased after deceit, Oh, let Him weigh me with accurate scales, And let God know my integrity. If my step has turned away from the way [of God], Or if my heart has [covetously] followed my eyes, Or if any spot [of guilt] has stained my hands," JOB 31:1-7 AMP

He was determined to overcome all challenges that may come along with his ministerial calling.

CHAPTER SEVEN

THE CALLED AND THE CHALLENGES

Within a short while, Donald was able to disciple and mentor Jeremiah into a Christian with acceptably good standing in the Lord. It was a common saying among the brethren that the spirit of Donald has fallen upon Jeremiah. He was almost a chip off the old block. There was no doubt that the hand of God was upon him. He was like Saul of Tarsus. He took Christianity as the only means of his survival in the conflicting world. Though he was a convert of Donald, his marital relationship won the admiration of his mentor. The secret prayer of Donald was that he would marry a woman like Abigail, the gift of God, in the life of Jeremiah. In his assessment of their temperamental disposition, Jeremiah was a melancholic sanguine while Abigail was a choleric melancholic, a very unusual temperamental combination that makes its possessor prone to mood-swing.

The spiritual growth of Jeremiah was very inspiring. His Area Pastor was fully persuaded that he was a material for pastoral ministry. He also was very eager to answer the calling of God. He had a personal conviction to be a full-time pastor. Though he had a very good job, he was ready to let go of everything for his service to the Lord. He was a ready material for the fulfillment of the vision of the Mission. He was invited by his District Pastor for a discussion on his conviction to break new grounds for the church. He had expressed his personal conviction to start a branch of the church in a remote town where the church does not exist. The discussion was very brief as they both were on the same page on the issue. The only contention was on the stand of the church concerning his job. The District Pastor was not ready to agree that Jeremiah should resign from his job. He preferred that he shuttles between Mexicana and Marlboro because that would save the church the responsibility of paying him any salary but allowance.

The work on the newly planted church in Marlboro took off with a speed that was beyond the comprehension of the pastor and ministers. There was no doubt that the Lord had gone ahead of the team to prepare the ground. Jeremiah was convinced of the necessity to resign from his full-time job to face the task of the ministry. There was no problem until the demonic kingdoms of darkness in the town were devastated by the ferocious prayers of Jeremiah, his wife and the prayer-band of the church. The spiritual atmosphere of the town was very conflicting. Jeremiah and his team were invited by the chiefs and

the powers that be. He was rugged and very uncom-
promising. The allegations were of no clear understanding to those that were spiritually ignorant.
Jeremiah had the insight to the intent of the meeting.
At the close of the discussion he informed the sitting
that the core of the discussion is spiritual. He cautioned
that all occultists in the land should desist from
supernormal powers and surrender their lives to Jesus.

The statement of Jeremiah unveiled the hidden core
of the contentions. One of the representatives of the
cult in the land challenged him to a spiritual
confrontation. He claimed that the gods of the land
had been around from time immemorial and that it
was Jeremiah and his intrusive forces that will have to
vacate the town for peace to reign. Ironically, his
statement gave Jeremiah some measure of confidence
that his prayers had made tremendous impact in the
realm of the spirit over the entire town. With a very
broad smile that expressed his confidence in the Lord,
he said: "The light shines in darkness and the
darkness comprehended it not." His statement was
like a ball of fire into a tank of gasoline. Jeremiah and
his wife were surprised to realize that almost
everyone at the meeting belonged to the occult. They
rose as if about to launch an attack. In unison they
chanted: "We shall know; 'who has the authority, the
farmer or the raccoon." The meeting was brought to
an abrupt end.

Though spiritually bold, Jeremiah was a little scared. He remembered some of the statements of his pastor: "Though well trained and prepared, no soldier desires going to war but has no choice when the battle line is drawn. A soldier is hired to kill or be killed." His thought was complimented by his wife as she said: "Jesus commanded the disciples to go; he did not tell them that they would return. We have come, the task must be done. My dear, we shall surely win this battle. I am happy you told them that darkness cannot overpower the light." Her statement pumped a measure of adrenaline into his blood stream. He held her hands and they went into a very intense prayer session. They surely took authority over the entire town and the forces in control. They determined to do spiritual mapping of the entire town. They prayed specific prayers on each of the locations.

Jeremiah had relocated his entire family to Marlboro. The church experienced a momentary setback. The spiritual warfare became very tensed. Things were hard for the survival of the family. The children were bullied in school and the neighborhood. Their first son was under a very challenging health issue. Though challenged, they held to the text that sparked the heat:
"The Light shines on in the darkness, and the darkness did not understand it or overpower it or appropriate it or absorb it [and is unreceptive to it]."
John 1:5 AMP.

The speedy recovery of Troy gave them the assurance that the Lord was on their side. Turning to his wife, he said, "I guess the Lord was trying to assure us that He is fighting our battles. All we need to do is to keep the fire burning." As he instructed:

"The fire shall be burning continually on the altar; it shall not [be allowed to] go out."Leviticus 6:13 AMP

His wife, with some stern look and a measure of righteous indignation, suggested that they change the style of their prayers. They agreed to call on their physical and spiritual allies for back-up. Jeremiah was reluctant to pray any imprecatory or vengeful prayers. In his opinion, they were in the town to win the souls of the people to the Lord. His wife was of a contrary view. She claimed that the Egyptians did not repent until they saw the hands of God in operation against them. She called his attention to the prayers of King David in Psalm 35. In her characteristic shout, she screamed: "Lord, visit the camp of our enemies and save us, our children and congregation in the mighty name of our Lord and Savior Jesus Christ." She was surprised that her husband responded with a very resounding "Amen".

One would have to agree that the opinion of his wife triggered his aggression against their awkward and frustrating experience, especially of the children. He could not understand why their children were being oppressed and bullied around town. Turning to his wife, he said: "I believe I am being led to pray some dangerous prayers against the enemies of our lives, especially the forces that have chosen to torment us by afflicting our children." Abigail was very happy that her husband had agreed to pray her usual but his very unusual type of prayers. She concluded that the forces of darkness and their agents in the town were in serious trouble.

Most of the days, they could not afford to sleep throughout the night. They spent a sizable time of the nights in spiritual warfare. At midday, Jeremiah was woken up from his little hangover of the night. He had had a very scary dream about their children in school. He opened his eyes and alas, it was supposed to be a dream. He immediately went into spiritual warfare, returning every force of affliction to the sender. He covered their children with the blood of Jesus Christ. He was very specific to demand the hand of God on the enemies of their souls.

At the close of the school day, Abigail was in the school to pick up the children when she saw the fire trucks and ambulances in the school premises. They were busy working on how to revive four of the students who were said to be having some unexplainable convulsions. She was a little inquisitive to know the names of the affected children. She realized that two of the children belonged to the man that first challenged them at the town-council meeting. She was not able to identify the two others. With gratitude to God, she gracefully picked her children and headed for their home. She viewed the development as an unfortunate situation until she got back home. She narrated the scenario to her husband. She was expecting his usual sympathetic response to horrific situations. Strangely, she heard her husband shout, "Thank you Jesus, thank you Jesus." He narrated to his wife, the divine revelation he had prior to the development in the school. He claimed that he saw the hands of death trying to pick their two children as they sat in the classroom. He remembered seeing two angels shielding the children away from the assailants. His shout: "Return to the sender" diverted the demonic claws away from their children to another direction. She was shocked. She conclusively said: "I pray the children should not die." Later in the day, the catastrophe that hit the school was in the news. Three of the four children were reported dead. The only survivor of the four was the daughter of one of their new converts in the church.

Abigail was a little scared of her husband's declarations. She cautioned him not to always pray prayers of imprecations. She was of the conviction that it was his prayers that killed the three children. He told his wife not to ever tell anybody that he prayed the death of the children. He claimed that the incident was an aversion. The occultist parents of the dead children knew that the incident was the consequence of their preplanned affliction on the family of Jeremiah and Abigail. They soon discovered that the father of the only survivor of the attack was the daughter of a former member of their cult with whom they still had contention over the salvation of his soul. In their anger, they determined to kill the little girl. They claimed her father would use her survival as a testimony against them. Mysteriously the little girl took ill. The doctors did their best to save her life but her condition was just deteriorating. In a trance, Abigail saw the girl struggling for survival in the hands of the enemies of her parents. An angel appeared and delivered the girl from their hands. When she opened her eyes, she was surprised that it was not a reality.

Abigail notified her husband of the divine revelation. They made a call to the father of the girl and they were informed that the girl and her parents were at the emergency section of the hospital. They rushed out of the house. They were few minutes to the hospital when they had a flat tire. Jeremiah was prompted to leave his wife with the car while he hurried to the hospital to pray for the girl. His arrival was timely. The doctors had just informed her parents that there was nothing they can do as the girl was to die any moment from then. Sighting Jeremiah, the parents shouted, "Praise the Lord you are here, please pray..." With righteous indignation, Jeremiah rebuked the spirit of death. He prayed thus:

"I come against every spirit of death.

You, the spirit of death, loose your hold on Deborah.

I set you the hands of death ablaze. Return to your sender.

Let the host of heaven destroy your root in Jesus' name.

I call Deborah back into the fullness of life.

I cancel every appointment with death. I turn her body into fire.

Holy Ghost fire, consume every form of infirmity and affliction in Jesus' name.

Holy Ghost fire, Fire, Fire, Fire..."

There was a sudden shaking on the bed. Deborah opened her eyes with ease and suddenly became radiant. She asked series of questions especially on why she was in the hospital. The doctors and nurses were surprised about the development. Jeremiah quickly directed their attention to the miracle working power of Jesus Christ. The doctor and two of the nurses determined to give their lives to Jesus. They asked for the address of the church. Jeremiah advised that they should find a living church closer to wherever they lived. He gave the counsel especially as he is aware that most of the doctors and nurses lived in the nearby big city. They however insisted that they would want to be in the church he attended. It was at that moment that he informed them that he was the pastor of the local parish of A-Z Holiness Church.

They all were excited to realize that he was a pastor. They assured him that they have already become members of his church.

The tire of the car had been fixed and Abigail just arrived in the hospital. She was conducted to the room where they all gathered sharing testimonies and exchanging pleasantries. She found Deborah talking and walking around. In her utmost surprise, she shouted: "Praise God, it is true." "What is true...?" Jeremiah questioned. "That the dead girl was raised back to life. I was told at the ground floor that a young girl was brought back to life by the fanatical pastor of the new church around town. "Abigail asserted. "To God be the glory, I never knew she was dead before we started praying..." The resident doctor who had just given his life to Jesus interrupted him: "We said, 'code blue' as you walked in. My colleague quickly walked away to avoid the prospective reaction of her parents. The information I gave them, that she may pass any moment from then, was for my escape from their tantrums. This your Jesus is a miracle working God. I promise to hold unto him forever. I have heard of diverse miracles. I doubted most of them, but I cannot deny this. Praise the Lord."

The news of the miracle stormed the entire town. Many came to the hospital to see the miracle girl and the "Black Jesus." The news went viral and many were anxious to know where the church was located. The popular nonsense of racial discrimination was completely drowned as people of diverse colors flooded the church at the mid-week service to see the miracle girl and possibly to get their much-desired personal miracles. The list of first-time attendees was the highest in the history of the church. Many of them decided to surrender their lives to Jesus. It was a spiritual boon (benefit) for the church.

The Holy Spirit whispered to the spirit man of Jeremiah that the entire church and especially him and his wife should intensify their prayers because the same spirit that worked in the lives of the injurious Jews in the days of Jesus was in operation in Marlboro. The Jews of old took counsel to kill Lazarus because he was the testimony of Jesus. The Bible says:

"A large crowd of Jews learned that He was there [at Bethany]; and they came, not only because of Jesus, but also to see Lazarus, whom He had raised from the dead. So the chief priests planned to kill Lazarus also, because on account of him many of the Jews were going away [from the teaching and traditions of the Jewish leaders] and believing in Jesus [following Him as Savior and Messiah]."John 12:9-11 AMP.

The church grew very rapidly, but most of the members did not have good jobs. Though they were taught to pay tithe out of their income, very few of them responded positively. The day to day running of the church became a serious burden on Jeremiah and his wife. Since he left his good paying job, they had to depend on the ministry for financial survival. The experience was not too pleasant especially as they decided to get a bigger space to accommodate the ever-increasing membership. Jeremiah appealed to the district office of the church for assistance, but nothing was forth coming. He decided to call on his immediate pastor and mentor, Donald. He was promised a little support. To make the urgency of the need obvious to Donald, he invited him to Marlboro for a ministerial visit and ministration. Donald honored the invitation. He went along with his promised support which was enough to pay the rent of the new location for about three months. The visit was good, and the ministration was wonderful. Donald was obviously very impressed when he saw the crowd. He found it difficult to believe that the church had the financial challenges as reported by their pastor.

As the practice of A-Z Holiness Church, members of the congregation were always encouraged to bless visiting ministers. The collection was wrapped up in a plastic-bag nicely packed in a fairly big envelope. It was sizably bulky. Donald was anxious to know the content of the gift. After his prayers on returning to his hotel room, he opened the envelope to count the money. He was immediately reminded of the song of a popular Christian artist;
Brother Chosen:-

"Give God Benjamin,
why give Him Washington,
Give God, give God, and give God Benjamin."

He smiled when he recalled the frustrations of the pastor that claimed he had banned "Washington" from coming to his church.

He burst into laughter when he remembered a purported conversation between One Dollar note [Washington] and One Hundred Dollar note [Benjamin].

Benjamin: "It's been a long while we met. Where have you been?

Washington: I have been in the church all this while. But I never saw you.

Benjamin: "My boss kept me busy at the marketplace. I may appear in the church on the New-Year eve or New-Year thanksgiving service if business permits."

He was not impressed to count the offering, but curiosity compelled him. He was disappointed when he realized that the offering could not settle his hotel bill. He now had a better understanding of the plight of Jeremiah. Sarcastically he soliloquized, "I hope these people will not get Jeremiah into Lamentation." At that moment he was grateful to God for his local church. Though they were not as many in number like the church of Jeremiah, they were professionals and faithfully committed to the cause of Christ. With a gratitude to God, he said: "Father, I thank you for bringing me here to reveal my ingratitude so as to change my Leviticus ineptitude through these convicting revelations."

Jeremiah visited his guest to show his appreciation. They had a good time of ministerial discussions. Donald was of the opinion that his host should do some series of teaching on "commitment to the cause of Christ." This he believed will enhance the financial state of the church. Just as they were about to close their meeting, Donald mentioned his concerns about the numerical strength of his local church. Jeremiah interrupted: "But they are doing well as evident by the finance of the church. You can comfortably meet all your needs. I have many times doubted whether God called me into the pastoral ministry. People have said, "if God gives a vision, He will also give the provision." I guess I have to rethink my calling. "Which other provision do you need for your ministry? Your real needed provision is the power to attract the people and disciple them for the kingdom. I wish I have what you have. You cannot afford to blame your tools; the initiative belongs to you. It is your duty to empower your members to be financially viable through productivity. However, it takes the grace of God."

Jeremiah felt convicted for ingratitude. He turned to his guest and said: "I guess you need to pray for me that the Lord may forgive me of my ingratitude." "I too." Donald interrupted. They joined their hands as they prayed fervently that the Lord would forgive them for their ingratitude. They both agreed to make the best of what the Lord had granted to them. Donald said: "I need to seek the face of the Lord for His miracle working power. I will also need you to visit my local church to talk to our brethren on the same theme but with emphasis on soul winning." With a broad smile Donald said: "You remember that our Area Pastor always says, "Make the best of what you have. The best is not that which you do not have. The best is, making the best of that which you have..." Jeremiah cut in: "Sir, you remember one of his stories of two guys that were jealous of each other's cross?" "O yes, the guy with the big wooden cross that coveted the smaller cross of the neighbor. They had the exchange before he realized that the smaller cross was a 'mercury-bank'." They both laughed. They realized that it is very important for every individual to make the best of whatever the Lord allows in his or her life. [Please learn to carry your own cross. Your cross is the challenges that you have to deal with.] Remember the statement of our Lord, Jesus Christ:

"Then Jesus said to His disciples, "If anyone wishes to follow Me [as My disciple], he must deny himself [set aside selfish interests], and take up his cross [expressing a willingness to endure whatever may come] and follow Me [believing in Me, conforming to

My example in living and, if need be, suffering or perhaps dying because of faith in Me]."
Matthew 16:24 AMP

They determined to work together to better their conditions by making the best of their situations. Their bonding was based on the scripture:
"As iron sharpens iron, so one man sharpens [and influences] another [through discussion]. He who tends the fig tree will eat its fruit, And he who faithfully protects and cares for his master will be honored. As in water face reflects face, so the heart of man reflects man."Proverbs 27:17-19 AMP

Donald returned to his local station, but could not get over the lessons the Lord taught him over the weekend. He took his Bible and read:

"For by the grace [of God] given to me I say to every one of you not to think more highly of himself [and of his importance and ability] than he ought to think; but to think so as to have sound judgment, as God has apportioned to each a degree of faith [and a purpose designed for service]. For just as in one [physical] body we have many parts, and these parts do not all have the same function or special use, so we, who are many, are [nevertheless just] one body in Christ, and individually [we are] parts one of another [mutually dependent on each other]. Since we have gifts that differ according to the grace given to us, each of us is to use them accordingly: if [someone has the gift of] prophecy, [let him speak a new message from God to His people] in proportion to the faith possessed; if service, in the act of serving; or he who teaches, in the act of teaching; or he who encourages, in the act of encouragement; he who gives, with generosity; he who leads, with diligence; he who shows mercy [in caring for others], with cheerfulness."Roman's 12:3-8 AMP

He was completely engrossed in thought about the marital relationship between Jeremiah and Abigail. In his observations about their relationship, he concluded that their unity was the very source of their spiritual success. He noted that the Bible says:
"How could one chase a thousand, And two put ten thousand to flight, unless their Rock had sold them, And the LORD had given them up?" Deut. 32:30 AMP
"Ascribe strength to God; His majesty is over Israel And His strength is in the skies."Psalms 68:34 AMP.

Loneliness had become a boredom to Donald. He determined to pray more fervently on the issue of marriage. He desired no woman lower in Christian virtues he had observed and admired in Sis. Abigail, the wife of his convert. He believed good married life enhances success in ministry.

==============================
"...Good married life enhances
success in ministry."
==============================

CHAPTER EIGHT

MARRIAGE AND MINISTRY

Pastor Rufus had schooled the youths in his church to value marriage next to eternity in heaven. He believed one can have a taste of heaven or hell through marriage while in this world. He claimed; "Marriage could be the onset of what he tagged "3D" Diversionary Device of the Devil." Most of the ideas that Donald had acquired about the concept of marriage were received during the period when he was the youth leader in the local church of Pastor Rufus. He strongly believed that one of the key pillars of a good marriage is personal confidence. His pastor once taught them that: "Anyone who has no confidence in himself or herself will be suspicious of his or her shadow."

Every youth in the church was mandated to make a good study of the subject of temperaments. They were to place anyone they wanted to relate with before the onset of the relationship. The idea greatly helped the youth fellowship and the entire church. According to Pastor Rufus, "You see first in others what you hate in yourself. That is the reason why opposites always attract each other because the individual would naturally seek what he or she lacked.

Donald, a melancholic-sanguine, needed a choleric personality to drive his 'slow-engine' but not to a halt. He had prayed well enough to hear from God. He was invariably waiting for God to give him the wife of his choice. He decided to meet his former pastor to seek counsel on the issue of his prospective marriage. His pastor had for a very long time desired to see him get married. One of his most disturbing puzzles was: "How will I know the lady when I meet her?" In his opinion, he was willing that God should choose for him. He was shocked when his pastor informed him that God would not choose for him but guide him to make the right choice. His surprise was evident on his face. His pastor questioned him whether he has any question. He responded: "Why would God not choose for me?" "Ok! You will notice that Adam blamed God when the devil successfully deceived Eve to breach divine instruction. Since then, God gave the liberty to man to find a wife of his choice."
The Bible says:
"He who finds a [true and faithful] wife finds a good thing And obtains favor and approval from the LORD." Proverbs 18:22 AMP

Pastor Rufus was determined to make sure that Donald was well guided on the issue of marriage. He said: "Pastor Donald, I am praying seriously that you marry a woman that will enhance your ministry. I have met many pastors whose ministries were destroyed or stagnated by the attitudes of their wives. Your calling is by now actually at a crossroad. We shall prayerfully look out for a sister that is the perfect will of God for you in marriage. God has His perfect will for you, but you must find her. When you find her, it is your duty to make her find fulfillment in your person. You have a great job to do as a man in ministry. The ministry and your calling begin from your home. Therefore you cannot afford a conflicting relationship."

Interestingly, Donald remembered that one of the sisters in the then youth fellowship had visited him few years back. In his wildest imagination, he could not see himself being accepted as a prospective husband by her. He believed her visit was only ministry related. He discouraged a repeat of the visit because he felt attracted to the very beautiful and highly educated sister. In his heart, he rebuked the devil. But that was more than three years ago. He could not imagine why his mind now went back to her. He narrated the entire experience to his pastor and mentor. The pastor was taken aback. He remembered that Sis. Ruth mentioned something like that to him about three years ago. He dismissed the idea because he felt that she was 'too-much' for him and more-so, as at then she did not look like a material for a pastor's wife. To him, she was too flashy. However, over the years, she had grown more matured as a Christian and better comported. As at the time of their discussion, Sis. Ruth had relocated to another city.

His pastor would have loved that Donald had a marital conviction for Ruth, but he was not sure whether she was fully convinced to marry Donald, after a three -year silence. He did not disclose to him [Donald] that she ever mentioned something of such. In his personal opinion, the will of God stands the test of time. Donald could not advance a good reason for his gravitation towards Ruth on marital inclination. He prayed and fasted. The more he prayed, the more he became restless on the issue.

He remembered that his pastor had taught them in the youth group that: "True love stands the test of time." He went for his notebook, flipping through the pages until he hit his mentor's teaching on the attributes of a good spouse.
It read:
1]. A good spouse must be fully convinced and persuaded to take the responsibility of his or her actions and experience, in the said relationship.
2]. A good spouse must be ready to give and aspire to give more.
3]. A good spouse must be led by the Spirit of God.
4]. A good spouse must be hard working.
5]. A good spouse must be sacrificial.

6]. A good spouse must be protective of his or her partner.

7]. A good spouse must be tolerant and accommodating.

8]. A good spouse must be respectful.

9]. A good spouse must be willing to obey God.

10]. A good spouse must have good knowledge of the word of God.

11]. A good spouse must be given unto prayers.

12]. A good spouse must be a catalyst.

13]. A good spouse celebrates the partner.

14]. A good spouse must price heaven higher than everything.

15]. The happiness of his or her partner must be his or her joy.

16]. A good spouse must necessarily have a good knowledge of the temperamental disposition of his or her spouse.

17]. A good spouse must have personal confidence so as to avoid paranoia.

Reading through his note, he concurred to the saying that, "The worst of pens is better than the best of brains."

In a soliloquy, he said: "Where is the good spouse?" He was quickly reminded: "The good makes things good." "The good are the pained. it takes deter-mination to be 'the good'". With a broad smile on his face, he toasted himself to be a good spouse. He recalled the moments when he had Ruth in their youth group. He tried to assess how much of these attributes she displayed. He could not come to a good conclusion. He had a very strong desire to meet her again.

Ruth had become a very committed worker in the parish where she worshipped. Her pastor had tried to connect her with a fervent brother in the church; she was not inclined. She believed that she was prepared to be the wife of a pastor. She had admired Donald when he was their youth leader. She visited him twice when he was "planted" out to pastor, the then new parish. She felt Donald was not interested in the subject of marital relationship. She believed strongly that she will pray her way through on her conviction. She had prayed that the will of God be done in her life. She decided to keep herself pure. She had since improved and developed herself in the Lord.

The teachings of Pastor Rufus had great impact on the youths that were in his church. Ruth, as taught in the youth group, believed that she should not sell herself cheap to any man, even in the expression of her convictions. She would rather settle her case on her knees. She always quotes her pastor and mentor: "Knee-benders are stronger than Iron-benders." It was as if the voice of her pastor was still speaking in her subconscious: "Don't ever love someone because of charisma but character. Don't ever marry because of materials possession, but based on Christian virtues. Relationship should not be based on emotional attachment but spiritual conviction. Any relationship that does not improve your Christian life will disapprove you before God. If you don't want to be bitter in life, don't sow bitterness into the lives of others. Make the happiness of the saints your joy..." In her assessment of herself and life determination, she believed she will make her husband happy.

Donald could not get over the cautions he had received from his pastor on the impact marriage could have on the ministry of "The Called." He had seriously cautioned him that:
"Any woman that cannot endure hardship is not suitable for "The Called".
A person that lacks initiative will over burden "The Called".
A spouse that nags and suffers from insecurity will be a clog in the wheel of progress of "The called."
A woman that cannot submit to her husband will ruin the calling of God.
A man that is not confident of God's grace in his personal life will ruin the calling and gifting of God in his wife.
"The Called" must be confident, tolerant, determined, resilient, innovative, loving, consistent, trustworthy and accommodating."

Pastor Rufus had a task to accomplish; how to reconnect to Sister Ruth. He tracked her through the pastor of one of the parishes in the city where Ruth was believed to reside. "Yes, I guess I know her," the pastor responded. Pastor Rufus was very excited. He felt he was on the right path to resolving the riddle on the prospective marriage of Donald, his dear son in the Lord. She was well reported by her pastor. Pastor Timothy however cautioned himself not to sing too much of her praise. He had suggested to her to be in a relationship with one of the brothers in his local church, but she declined. She said she will not get into any relationship until she gets to hear that the man of her conviction got married to someone else. She refused to disclose his identity. Pastor Timothy, in his conclusive statement said: "Sister Ruth Emmanuel is a very committed young lady. She is just an adamant character when it comes to holding to her convictions." "I guess her last name is Gamble," Pastor Rufus retorted. "May be there is a mix-up. The sister with us here is not Gamble but Emmanuel." His zeal was deflated; he felt very disappointed. He was no longer interested in the discussion. The conversation was ended.

Pastor Rufus was anxious to know whether she had had a change of name as she had on many occasions been taunted by her peers. Her response was always: "The name will change when I get married." He remembered that he had to resolve a conflict between her and one of the brethren who jokingly told her: "Why do you choose to "gamble" until you get

married? Marriage is not something you gamble with."
She took a very serious offense, and the matter had to
come before the pastor. That occasion actually made
the pastor to recognize her person. One good that the
conflict made on her was that she determined not to
gamble on the issue of who to marry. She was fully
convinced that Donald was to be her husband and
was ready to wait until he was ready or otherwise. Her
solace was in the scripture:

"Therefore the Lord GOD says this, "Listen carefully, I
am laying in Zion a Stone, a tested Stone, and A
precious Cornerstone for the [secure] foundation,
firmly placed. He who believes [who trusts in, relies
on, and adheres to that Stone] will not be disturbed or
give way [in sudden panic]." Isaiah 28:16 AMP

Donald was out of state; it was not possible for Pastor
Rufus to get to him. He decided to give him a call,
though he would have preferred a face to face
discussion. He eventually agreed to call him on
WhatsApp video call. "I am not aware of any change
of name," he responded. "When last did you discuss
with her?" "We have not had any discussions in more
than a year. However, I know how to link up with her
but; I don't know why I am now very shy to talk to
her." "Do you have any imagination about her
concerning marriage?" Pastor Rufus questioned. There
was silence. "Are you still there?," he further
questioned. "Sort of," came the melancholic voice.

"Please kindly find out if she had a change of name," he suggested.

Ruth's phone rang; it was a call from Donald. "Is that Sis. Ruth Gamble?" "Do you mean to talk to Ruth Emmanuel?" was the response. "That will be right if I am talking to the same person!" "Yes, you are" Ok! But you did not inform me that you changed your last name to my middle name. That is very interesting if not prophetic." Ruth shrugged in great surprise. She was the more shocked by the insinuation in the statement of Donald; "That is very interesting if not prophetic." It seemed to have said it all but neither of the two was ready to bell the cat. Donald was careful in his subsequent statements as he felt he was too direct, [at least that was how he felt in himself] on the most paramount issue of his intended relationship with Ruth. He said: "I just said I should hear your voice after a fairly long time." "You mean a very long time!" responded Ruth. "I guess I feel so too. Ok we will talk later," Donald concluded.

The call made her day. She could not get over the coded statements of Donald. She thought of the coincidence of her changing her last name to Emmanuel which happened to be the middle name of Donald. She became restless. She was anxious to know the very reason why he called. She felt her prayers were being answered but could not get any tangible clue to the desires of her heart being fulfilled. She wished her change of name had been prophetic. Her sleep departed from her. She decided to call her pastor to pray with her, yet without the disclosure of her consternation. After the prayers, the pastor asked whether she was ever addressed as Ruth Gamble. Her response got her Pastor to talk more. "Pastor Rufus was looking for you, but I told him that the Sister Ruth that I know does not go by the name Gamble. I was almost joking with him that the Ruth I know is very focused and led by her convictions without any iota of a gamble. I guess I like your new name Emmanuel [God with us.] God must have led you on the change of name to Emmanuel. She became a little more inquisitive: "Did he talk to you about any Emmanuel?" "No, I told him the Sis. Ruth that I know is Emmanuel's, a true child of God." "Amen." She shouted. Her pastor got the excitement in her response but had no clue to why. She keyed into the prophetic pronouncement of her pastor believing she shall become the wife of Donald Emmanuel O'rende. She took her Bible and read:

"For I know the plans and thoughts that I have for you,' says the LORD, 'plans for peace and well-being and not for disaster, to give you a future and a hope. Then you will call on Me and you will come and pray to Me, and I will hear [your voice] and I will listen to you."Jeremiah 29:11-12 AMP

She went on her knees and prayed fervently that the perfect will of the Lord should be done in her life. She petitioned God that He should put the love for her in the heart of Donald. She asked for God to give her the grace to be a good wife that will enhance his ministry and make them both finish well in the Christian race. God must have given her prayers an express response.

There was a dialogue between Pastor Rufus and Donald. He was very excited when he was told that Ruth Gamble was the same Ruth Emmanuel. Donald was quick to inform his mentor that Emmanuel happens to be his middle name. With excitement his pastor and mentor said: "I wish she still holds to her 'mini-convictions' of three years ago, that will make Emmanuel to be her name. "Sir, what was her conviction?" Donald excitedly asked. "Well, let's pray that the will of God be done in your life and ministry especially on the issue of marriage." The pastor cautioned.

Pastor Timothy and Pastor Rufus compared their notes. They realized that Ruth was holding to her convictions of many years awaiting Donald's recent conviction. Pastor Timothy had a very high respect for Ruth for holding to her said conviction without any contention with his contrary proposal. Her confession of assurance, any time Pastor Timothy asked her about a suitor was: "I know him, and I am sure God is preparing me for him and him for me."

Pastor Rufus was very happy that his mentee was going to marry a well discipled and disciplined lady who could keep herself pure and hold to her conviction for over a period of three years. Jokingly, Pastor Timothy said, "Sir, don't forget that her name is 'Ruth.' It is interesting that in most cases people act the implications or meaning of their names." They both laughed.

Arrangements were made by the two pastors to bring them both together. It was a brief meeting. Donald was more shy because he was just coming into a final conviction, but Ruth had been living in faith in expectation of the development. The two ministers prayed for and with them for the commencement of their courtship. It was the beginning of an onslaught against the devil.

Donald was anxious to ask Ruth about her visit to his station almost four years ago. Her response was: "I was there to spy on your liberty and liberality. You did not disappoint me by your sensitivity and stylish way of playing off the scene. It just gave me additional reinforcement that you are a self-disciplined young man. I really love you for it and prayed you into my life. I hope I made no mistakes." "I guess you do not have to question your conviction that had stood the test of time. I am the one to be sure that I have not made a mistake." With a smile,

Ruth responded: "God will surely help me to make you know that you have not made any mistake. I know I am not a mistake. Remember that our pastor and mentor always tell us: "God made everything but mistakes."

Their courtship lasted about seven months. Donald was the more anxious for the consummation of the relationship. The wedding date was fixed and perfectly solemnized. It was interesting that the presence of Ruth in the life of Donald attracted more people into the church. At a point, he had the feeling that some people joined the church for the confidence that he is now a married man. He could not charge them for any indictment or a cast of aspersion but to think they stayed away due to what he believed was their personal insecurity not based on any suspicion or dent on his own integrity and spiritual maturity.

The exchange of pulpit between Donald and Jeremiah was of great blessing to the two families and ministries. Ruth was able to understudy Abigail, an older friend and experienced house-wife who had been in the ministry with her husband for a while. Both women were given a measure of liberty and encouragement by their husbands. Ruth was more enthusiastic about evangelism and outreach than Abigail. She believed she was called by God to stand by her husband to bring more souls to the saving grace of Jesus Christ. It was the responsibilities of her husband to disciple them. She, a strong choleric, had little or no tolerance for the errors of many of the brethren. She questioned the salvation of their souls, an inquiry that her husband always responded: "Did you die for them? They will surely grow into spiritual-maturity." In most cases they both laughed over the issue of authenticity of the salvation of the souls of some of the brethren in the church.

Pastor Donald had his consolation in the letter of Apostle Paul to the Galatians: "My little children, for whom I am again in [the pains of] labor until Christ is [completely and permanently] formed within you— how I wish that I were with you now and could change my tone, because I am perplexed in regard to you."Galatians 4:19-20 AMP

He called some of the disobedient ones, "wonderful brethren", and a statement to which his wife always strongly objected. He consoled her that he was prophesying into their lives. He claimed he held to Apostle Paul's declaration:

"(as it is written [in Scripture], "I HAVE MADE YOU A FATHER OF MANY NATIONS ") in the sight of Him in whom he believed, that is, God who gives life to the dead and calls into being that which does not exist." Romans 4:17 AMP.

Ministry was very exciting to them both. Donald had great confidence in his wife. He encouraged her to get involved in preaching in the church. She had her biases about some of the brethren. She may not preach a sermon without referring to some of the known errors of the brethren. Her sermons were always very contemporary. Many of the brethren believed that she was always preaching about them. Some lodged their complaints with her husband whom they regarded as their pastor. In their opinion, she was the pastor's wife. The contention was brewing hot in some quarters; Donald had a big lump to swallow. He could understand the relevance of the style of her preaching but many of the brethren did not. Some who had confided in their Pastor believed that he must have shared the issue of their lives with his wife and that could be the only source of her knowledge about them as reflected in her sermon. One or two families left the church on the account of related issues. Donald was not too comfortable with the development. He was however matured enough not to allow the ministry to conflict with his home.

The church was blessed and the brethren did not hear Ruth preach too often. Her husband had played it safe to engage her in outreach programs. She was encouraged to plant new parishes, a suggestion which had been her heart desire. She was always away from home. Her return was always celebrated by those who enjoy her effervescence. Her bubbling and evangelistic babbling were of great fun even to her distractors who must have had a relief in her absence. She became the spice of her husband's ministry. It will not be outrageous to say everybody loved her. Her weaknesses were carefully concealed by her husband. It was obvious that the brethren had accepted her evangelistic approach to her church involvements she could talk; blabbing over some issues and get away with it. Whenever she was away, most of her admirers looked sad in the church. She was almost becoming their adrenalin infusion. They enjoyed her dancing and excitement compared to the melancholic life-style of her husband, their pastor.

Ruth was very confident of the discipline and spiritual maturity of her husband. She had some air of freedom for him during counseling sessions with female members of the church. She strongly believed that she was good enough for everything her husband could want from a woman. She endorsed Apostle Paul's statement:

"The husband must fulfill his [marital] duty to his wife [with good will and kindness], and likewise the wife to her husband. The wife does not have [exclusive] authority over her own body, but the husband shares with her; and likewise the husband does not have [exclusive] authority over his body, but the wife shares with him. Do not deprive each other [of marital rights], except perhaps by mutual consent for a time, so that you may devote yourselves [unhindered] to prayer, but come together again so that Satan will not tempt you [to sin] because of your lack of self-control."1 Corinthians 7:3-5 AMP

Though she did not infringe on her husband's liberty with female members of the church, she was very sensitive to the insinuations of some of the ladies. Her husband was aware of her style of cautioning him about any lady with whom she was not comfortable. Their relationship was the envy of many.

Concerning other men, Donald was jealous of the beauty of his wife. He would stylishly warn her of undue liberty or intimacy with other male ministers. In return, she also taunted him: "Keep your calm; it is not a crime to be beautiful. God prepared you for me and kept me for you. You had my virginity and would always have me. If you want me to stay home for ever, I will. You may just always need analgesic balm." Their relationship was hitch free until they started raising children. They have been taught that children are part of the ministry, for any Christian parent. It is a tougher task for those that are called into pastoral or evangelistic ministry.

Pastor Donald and Evangelist Ruth were well schooled about the challenges of children in the ministry. Her gestation period posed a little challenge to the inexperienced couple. Ruth displayed diverse unusual traits. She complained virtually about everything. She detested many things and at a particular time she could eat anything. She, at another time, was weary and very choosy about what she would want to eat. At odd times of the day or night, she demanded for items that were not accessible or affordable. It was too stressful for Donald. He made a call to his convert and marital mentor. He remembered the teaching of his pastor and mentor, Pastor Rufus; that every newly wedded needs a marital mentor especially when 'new grounds' are opening and a new layer of the 'matrimonial onion' unfolds. He was nicely counseled. He learnt to do everything humanly possible to please his wife during her period of pregnancy. At the close of the counseling session, Jeremiah said: "You will be blessed if your wife is not very prone to nausea [vomiting] in early pregnancy. If she is, get ready to take a better care. Be ready to pack her vomits or get the bowl ready for any throw-up." Donald laughed but Jeremiah cautioned him that it may not be funny. At the close of the session, he was prepared to be a husband with better understanding. He remembered Pastor Rufus' statement: "The anointing flows better when your spouse is happy with you. You minister the fivefold ministry empowerment, God the Father, God the Son, God the Holy Spirit, You and Your Spouse." With a broad smile he entered into his car and drove straight home in anticipation of his practicals.

He ruminated on Apostle Paul's statement:

"But I want you to be free from concern. The unmarried man is concerned about the things of the Lord, how he may please the Lord; but the married man is concerned about worldly things, how he may please his wife, and his interests are divided. The unmarried woman or the virgin is concerned about the matters of the Lord, how to be holy and set apart both in body and in spirit; but a married woman is concerned about worldly things, how she may please her husband. Now I say this for your own benefit; not to restrict you, but to promote what is appropriate and secure undistracted devotion to the Lord."
1 Corinthians 7:32-35 AMP.
He soliloquized: "The Lord will surely give me the grace and ability to cope with these additional responsibilities."

Though grateful to God for the pregnancy, she was not happy that she could not meet up with her regular ministerial commitments. She was greatly encouraged by her husband. She determined to make the best of her time. She did a lot of follow-up and wrote many tracts in the course of her pregnancy. Her doctor informed her that she was going to give birth to a set of twins. In one of the evenings as they returned from the mid-week service, Donald was to assist his wife in the preparation of the dinner. He noticed that she was about to throw-up. He could not find a bowl nearby, but quickly shaped his two hands into a cup and received the vomit so that her dress was not soiled, or the carpet stained. She looked at him with a great awe and admiration. That singular action endeared him to her heart.

At the time of her delivery, she was delivered of triplet, contrary to the doctor's report that she was carrying a set of twins. The unprepared, inexperienced couple was blessed with two identical boys and a girl. It was a moment of sadness and joy. Though excited, they could not figure out how to take care of the children. Ruth felt all her ministerial involvements were about to get completely disrupted or destroyed. In her determination for ministerial effectiveness, arrangements were made to bring her mother in, to help the family care for the triplet. She created other ministerial areas of involvement for herself. She graduated from writing tracts to writing manuals for the various arms of the church. According to her, God's blessings should not be allowed to be any form of obstruction to divine mandate.

As the ministry grew, it was as if all objections and oppositions were directed at the pastor's wife and children. Every gesture of the pastor's wife was given an undue interpretation or implication. It took the pastor a lot of wisdom to navigate the very dark and slippery ally of members and ministers' criticism of the pastor's wife and children. On one occasion, the pastor's wife determined to vent her feelings without ruffling the feathers of the saints. She sarcastically said: "My children and I are the most important people in this church; reason why we are always the center of most discussions. No one spends his or her time on anything that is not of importance." Everybody laughed. A sizable number of the congregants got the message in her sarcasm.

With her characteristic choleric lifestyle she success-fully waded through the challenges of ministry and marriage.

Deaconess Ruth, as she was newly ordained, expressed her appreciation to the entire congregation on their return from the annual convention of the church during which she was ordained. She was heartily congratulated by some of the brethren while some of her distractors felt the ordination was just to fuel her egocentricity which they claimed was peculiar to her temperamental disposition. She was not badly affected by the attitude of some of the brethren. In some instances, she felt that her husband gave preference to members of the church to her detriment. She purposed in her heart that she will not allow the ministry to have adverse effects on her marriage. She understood the spirituality and delicacy of their callings. She took her Bible to verify a verse of the scripture:

"The wise woman builds her house [on a foundation of godly precepts, and her household thrives], But the foolish one [who lacks spiritual insight] tears it down with her own hands [by ignoring godly principles]. He who walks in uprightness [reverently] fears the LORD [and obeys and worships Him with profound respect], But he who is devious in his ways despises Him." Proverbs 14:1-2 AMP.

She nodded her head in approval, as she closed the door of her room.

There were some members of the Board of Trustee of the church who have arrogated more power to themselves than expected. They tended to control the pastor. It was a thing of great concern to Deaconess Ruth. She determined to sort things out at her place of prayer.

CHAPTER NINE

THE POWER OF PRAYER

Prayer is a dialogue between God and man. God is a good listener who has knowledge prior to the dialogue. He is aware of the causes of the challenges and the solution to the problems. Prayer is a partial fulfillment of the purpose for which God created man. He loves to communicate with man. This was reflected in the book of Genesis:

"And they heard the sound of the LORD God walking in the garden in the cool [afternoon breeze] of the day, so the man and his wife hid and kept themselves hidden from the presence of the LORD God among the trees of the garden. But the LORD God called to Adam, and said to him, "Where are you?"
Genesis 3:8-9 AMP

Donald and his wife had learnt a lot from their mentors and converts about the importance of prayer in the handling of spiritual matters; especially in the leadership of the church and ministries. Donald grew in the ministry with the notion that a prayer-less Christian is a powerless Christian. He was told that prayerlessness is a display of pride against God. He strongly believed that many Christians get into troubles because the issues involved were not taken to the Lord at the place of prayer. Should anything unwholesome or negative happen, his first question was always: Where did I miss it? Have I presented this issue before God? What would God have me to do that I have neglected?" These principles had kept him going in the ministry since he came in contact with mentors that the Lord planted in his life.

Ruth made some observations about the personal comportment and insinuations of one of the female members of the church towards her husband. It was a difficult situation that she needed all God's wisdom at her disposal to handle. She trusted her husband well enough to believe that he would not be involved in any scandal with the lady. She at the same time, determined not to take chances or be negligent. She spoke to her husband about the lady but her husband could not reason in the same line with her on the issue. He assured her that he will never allow any woman to pull him down or dent his testimony by casting any suspicion or aspersion on his personality. Ruth's suspicions were true, but the lady was very clever as she tied her illicit intentions to her ministerial and clerical duties in the church. She was a "bee" in the relationship of the pastor and his wife.

It was good that Mommy Pastor Rufus had schooled the female youths in those good old-days. Then, Ruth was a member of their local church. She diligently taught them to fight for their husbands on their knees. She went into serious spiritual warfare; and prayed that the Lord should rekindle the fire of love for her in the heart of her husband. She commanded the angels of God to shield her husband from the strategies of any strange woman or the so called "grateful women." She laid special emphasis on the person of the lady by name. She commanded her counsel to be turned into foolishness. The most interesting part of her prayers was that; "The Lord should do something good to the lady so that she will never focus on her husband; but peradventure she refuses to repent, the Lord should paint her with ugliness that would make her husband to abhor and detest her." Within a short while she noticed that the lady was a little withdrawn from her usual activities in the church. She made some mistakes that made the ministerial team of the church to demand a sanction against her. It was not long when she informed the pastor and his wife that she got a new job that compelled her relocation. Ruth was excited to pray with her on her departure. No one had the least idea that she was instrumental to her "fortune" or predicaments.

At dinner in one of the evenings, Ruth jokingly teased her husband: "How is the church office since Sister Jazzy left for her new job out of state?" Her husband heaved a great sigh and said: "I guess, women are the most sensitive of God's creation. I did not see what you saw when you cautioned me about her. I was actually offended by your cautionary observations but desired not to vent my feelings. When the reality dawned on me, I was ashamed of my coming to talk to you about it. Your prior caution strengthened my determination and self-fortification to shield myself off her evil intentions." He stood up from his meal, reached for his office bag and brought a card Jazzy sent to him on his birthday. It read: "Dear Pastor Donald, it is nice having the privilege of coming around you. It may interest you to know how much of a blessing you have been in my life. I very much appreciate your love for Christ. I am only a little apprehensive of your insensitivity to my special interest in your love for God's creativity and variety. I hope to get better involved in your next birthday fun. Happy Birthday to a Darling Pastor." Ruth was silent for a while. Her silence was broken by a question from her husband: "Did you get the message in the card?" "Well, the content was carefully worded to avoid indictment but it did not leave out suspicions," she responded, "You are very right. I got her message and insinuation clearly. From that very moment, I plugged all loop holes of her access to me. She felt offended. More especially as I did not acknowledge the card and a fairly fat check... guess how much? Two thousand dollars and thirty-five cents." With her hand over her mouth, his wife said: "And what did you do with the check?" "It was recorded with all the gifts." I guess you only counted the money but you did not check the records of who gave what?" he lightly indicted her. "Well, I was not out to audit but to keep record." They both laughed.

Ruth was very thankful to God for answered prayers. The experience made her believe that with God, nothing shall be impossible.

She took her Bible and read:

"Then Moses said to the people, "Do not be afraid! Take your stand [be firm and confident and undismayed] and see the salvation of the LORD which He will accomplish for you today; for those Egyptians whom you have seen today, you will never see again. The LORD will fight for you while you [only need to] keep silent and remain calm."Exodus 14:13-14 AMP

Donald was very thrilled with the story of the spiritual warfare and battle strategy his wife adopted in the course of the conflicting opinion about Jazzy. With a muse she said: Thank God for the life of Pastor Grace Okonrende, especially for her book, "Pastor's wife praying manual" I got my strategy from the book and it worked. My knowledge of that book had been principally responsible for my personal comportment since I read it." "Praise the Lord for such books... can I also read it?" "Are you a pastor's wife? Anyway, I guess it is very important that men also read it, at least it will give them an idea of our expectations and untold pains, and if not hardship we pass through."

She handed him the book. He was actually expecting a voluminous book as his wife had expressed the magnitude of its impact. "I guess I can finish this in an hour!" "That is the whole idea about its size and impact," she responded. They had a wonderful night.

Everything was working out fine in the ministry and the church as a whole. It was always the practice of the prayer team of the church to meet for intercessory prayers every Thursday of the week and join the entire church to pray at night vigils on Fridays. It was a very powerful arm of the church. The team was led by a very dynamic young man, Bro Nathaniel. He worked hand in hand with an old lady in the church popularly called Mama Eunice. She was over seventy-five years old. She had been an intercessor since her youth. Her husband was over eighty years old when he passed into glory. He was largely sustained by her prayers over a long period of time. He was the oldest person to ever live that long with a blood disorder. Mama Eunice was a pillar in the church. The pastor would have made her the functional head of the prayer ministry of the church but for the paper-work, energy and rigor required. She was always deferred to when it came to what and how to pray. Her popular chapter of the scripture was Luke 18. She quoted almost the whole chapter from memory. Her point of emphasis was:

"Now Jesus was telling the disciples a parable to make the point that at all times they ought to pray and not give up and lose heart, saying, "In a certain city there was a judge who did not fear God and had no respect for man. There was a [desperate] widow in that city and she kept coming to him and saying, 'Give me justice and legal protection from my adversary.' For a time he would not; but later he said to himself, 'Even though I do not fear God nor respect man, yet because this widow continues to bother me, I will give her justice and legal protection; otherwise by continually coming she [will be an intolerable annoyance and she] will wear me out.'" Then the Lord said, "Listen to what the unjust judge says! And will not [our just] God defend and avenge His elect [His chosen ones] who cry out to Him day and night? Will He delay [in providing justice] on their behalf? I tell you that He will defend and avenge them quickly. However, when the Son of Man comes, will He find [this kind of persistent] faith on the earth?""
Luke 18:1-8 AMP

It was the strong belief of Pastor Donald that the church cannot survive without prayers. He remembered the statement of E. M. Bounds: "Prayers outlive the lives of those who uttered them; outlive a generation, outlive an age, outlive a world" He held ardently to the opinion that prayer is the mainstream and mainstay of any Christian ministry. He had very high regards for Mama Eunice. He took special interest in her well-being. She got special treats at occasions and special events. Her gifts at every Christmas were always special. She was a gem to the entire church but a special person to the Donald O'Rende's family. Her birthday was always graced with intercessory prayers for all ministers of the gospel. She believed that 'Pastors and their families are always the first target of the devil in his battle against the church.' The church was well known for the power of prayers. Many of the passersby called the church "the AMEN church" because of the resounding "AMEN" after every word of prayer.

Pastor Donald would do anything possible to protect his faith in Christ and the objects of his calling. He had always been a marriage counselor. According to him, that was his primary calling before his pastor 'coopted' him into the pastoral ministry in which he had excelled over the years. He conducted marriage seminars in his local church and many city-wide marriage counseling sessions. He was of the opinion that good knowledge of one's partner and the word of God coupled with prayers will afford any couple a happy home. One of his members once asked him at a seminar: "Sir, what do I do to my in-laws who have refused to allow peace in our home?" His answer was, "Find out who they are, love and pray for them." The guy came up with another question: "Supposing they choose not to be placated or pacified?" "Give more, love and pray for them." "Pastor, you do not seem to have any idea of how difficult to please, they have been." His response was: "Love and pray for them. Always understand that whatever the Holy Spirit cannot resolve, man cannot undo." He very much believed in the efficacy of prayer.

He quoted:
"Rejoice always and delight in your faith; be unceasing and persistent in prayer; in every situation [no matter what the circumstances] be thankful and continually give thanks to God; for this is the will of God for you in Christ Jesus. Do not quench [subdue, or be unresponsive to the working and guidance of] the [Holy] Spirit." 1 Thessalonians 5:16-19 AMP.

Grandma Eunice was getting very old. The children were out of state. It was their desire to have their mother around them in efforts to give her every necessary care and attention especially at the demise of her husband. She had to leave the church. There was a little get together in her honor, pending departure from the church. She had nurtured the church to an appreciably good standard at the place of prayers on her knees. It was not a send-off party. Pastor Donald emphatically informed the gathering that they were not sending Grandma Eunice off but she was being sent forth. It was a gathering, evident of mixed feelings. Many were very disturbed that the old lady was going out of their physical proximity. Others felt it was a good move by the children to give their mother a good treat in her old age. Pastor Donald in his opinion was satisfied that the children chose not to send their mother to old-people's home but to take personal care of their treasured gem, who had spent a sizable part of her life taking care of them. Though he would not want her to leave the church, he however had to agree in the interest of her good comfort at old age. He believed that there is no distance in the realm of the spirit as the church would still continue to enjoy the benefits of her endearing prayer life.

In his soliloquy, with a squint and a tincture of smile, he said aloud; "My only concern is for her beautiful garden that she had maintained with every meticulous attention and affection for the plants." Everybody around him laughed. The laughter caught the attention of Grandma Eunice who was oblivious of the cause of the laughter. Pastor Donald, with a very broad smile turned, speaking directly to her said: "I was lost in thought not realizing when I expressed my pity for your plants at your relocation." Grandma Eunice responded with her eyes laced with tears as she said: "I am pleased to realize that I am not the only one that felt for the plants. I know my children have a great plan for their care for me. Probably none of them thought of the plants in my garden. I can take my animate pets along but what happens to the inanimate. My departure from you all is not as painful as parting with my treasured garden. You can take care of yourselves but my plants need every help from me to survive. My children are yet to tell me the plans they have for the property. I wish my plants can go with me." Everybody laughed. The laughter was abruptly halted when she said with all seriousness. "It's not funny." Her reaction actually sent the message that plants have life and can react to hunger, negligence and abandonment.

Comfort is always the desire of every living being; however it could be a subtle destroyer. Grandma Eunice's relocation did not have any obvious impact on the church. Only those who had emotional attachment to her actually felt her absence. The realm of the spirit did not notice any difference because she did not relent in her efforts in praying for the church. She was always in good contact with the pastors and ministers of the church through the phone and social media. She did not miss the weekly prayer tele-conference. Everything was going on smoothly. She had no additional responsibility that makes a demand of a wipe of sweat. Her only duty was to see to the wellbeing of her grandchildren whose company she enjoyed as it broke the monotony of her sitting before the television screen. On a regular basis, she watched her endless Christian channel programs when she was outside of her prayer room.

She soon gained some weight as she burnt less calories everyday. She remembered her good time with her plants. Her attempt to work in the garden was viewed as a degrading line of action and an obstruction to the duties of the hired gardeners who took care of the lawns and garden.

To Grandma Eunice, life was boring without any activity that will compel her to burn some energy. She pleaded with her children to register her in the nearest gym so that she could go there for fitness exercises. Her request was handled with negligence and levity. The children felt it was going to be a waste of time and funds. Her only source of exercise was her occasional prayer-walk in the neighborhood, a practice that did not win the approval of her children. They felt it was not safe for her as the neighborhood was adjudged not safe enough for her strolls. She determined to make the best of her boredom. She set out to write some Christian tracts which she sent to her very much-loved church for printing and publication for evangelism. She wrote close to five hundred tracts on various subject matters, all pointing the reader to Jesus Christ. Age was actually telling on her. She could have had a better physical condition if she was granted the liberty to burn her energy on some physical activities.

It was already four years that Grandma Eunice has been tied down to the apron of indulgent comfort. She started complaining of minor illnesses and ailments. Her joints were not as strong as they used to be. She complained of general weakness of the body. Suddenly she laughed hysterically. Her daughter in-law questioned her laughter. She responded: "I just remembered one of the occasions when I was the matron in-charge of St. Monica High School. It was a standard practice that English language must remain the medium of expression in the school. There was a young girl in her first year, which had very little knowledge of the language. She came to my office to complain about her state of health. She said: "Excuse me, Ma, I am not feeling fine. I do not know what exactly is wrong with me. I have high temptation and general wickedness of the body." She meant to say; high temperature and general weakness of the body". The daughter in-law burst into laughter. "Now you know why I laughed," she retorted. They both laughed together. It was always fun staying with Grandma Eunice. There was never a boring moment with her but loneliness, an experience she converted to sweet hours of prayers. The grandchildren desired to always be around her because she told them very animating old stories.

Grandma took ill. It was very brief. She called her children together after a dinner. She made a valedictory speech that was least taken by her children, grandchildren and in-laws as a final discussion with them. She was heard praying fervently few minutes before she called for the family altar as was her usual practice every evening since she got into their home. They all prayed together and wished Grandma a stronger and better health. She turned to her son who had not been a stable Christian. She said: "I guess you will decide to take your Christianity more seriously when the pastor preaches at my funeral." Bruce responded with his usual humor: "I am serious but not just serious enough for your liking." "Not my liking but the Lord's approval that matters. What exactly is your role in the church of Christ? Realize you have not been a stable member of any particular church. When you were much younger, you told me that the Lord would want you to be a chorister and a teacher in the Sunday school. I told you, you have all it takes to be a pastor. My surprise is the fact that the zeal of your youthful days had disappeared into despair. I pray you will wake up to fulfill purpose." "I will surely fulfill my purpose in the Lords vineyard in Jesus mighty name." His mother said a very resounding Amen. She embraced him as she said good night. See you tomorrow.

As usual, Bruce expected to see his mother at the living room in the morning as was her practice. He knocked at the door of her room but no response was heard. He opened the door and found his mother on her knees. He felt he should not disturb or obstruct her prayers. He left for his office. It was the holiday season. The grandchildren expected their grandma to have woken them up for the usual Morning Prayer (family altar.) With curiosity, they went into her room and saw her still on her knees. They also decided not to disturb her at the place of prayer. At mid-day, Bruce called from work to check on his praying mother. His wife who was off duty for the day went into grandma's room. She noticed she was not making the usual sounds. She went closer, she discovered she was motionless. She attempted to pull her up. Alas Grandma had passed on into glory. She screamed, and all the grandchildren ran to her. They all realized that Grandma was dead. She died on her knees. Bruce was quickly informed. He rushed home. He shook his mother, tried all his medical skills to bring her back to life, but to no avail. "She had gone to be with her Lord. She prayed her way into heaven," he asserted.

The whole church of A-Z Holiness Church was greatly aggrieved at the death of Grandma Eunice. They felt the big blow of her demise but could not appreciate well enough the consequence or implication of her death on the church. The funeral of Grandma Eunice Thomas attracted all and sundry. Bruce could not get over the shock, especially the seemingly valedictory speech of his mother. He felt he must honor his mother by his commitment to the cause of Christ.

Just about six months after the death of Grandma Eunice, Pastor Donald observed that there were many contentions in the church, such that caused a great drift of many of the members. He was greatly disturbed. He went to the Lord in prayers and fasting. He engaged the prayer team of the church in series and sessions of prayers. It was revealed to him that the challenging situation was the consequence of the "vacuum" created by the death of Grandma Eunice. Though it was not difficult for him to believe. Same revelation was given to two other members of the prayer band of the church. They were instructed to bridge the gap to forestall further activities of the devil in the church. When Pastor Donald revealed the divine information given to him and the necessary lines of action to take in order to enforce spiritual sanity in the church, the other members of the team completely concurred. They engaged in regular prayer sessions for the restoration and elevation of the church. Before long, the church was able to sail and soar high in the realm of the spirit with evident results in the numerical growth of the church.

It became very obvious to Pastor Donald that prayer is the principal pillar for the sustenance of his calling. He determined not to take the issues of prayer lightly. There is no doubt that Lucifer and his cohorts do not make cheap choices. His young but exciting marriage experienced some challenges. His wife and himself had some cold wars. Things were no longer as usual. It was difficult for him to confide in any member of the church though he had many experienced elderly married couples with him. He preferred to seek the face of the Lord and the counsel of his parents in the Lord. He could not imagine the implication of seeking the assistance of members of his local church. He reached for his Bible and read: "Like a broken tooth or an unsteady foot is confidence in an unfaithful man in time of trouble. Like one who takes off a garment in cold weather, or like [a reactive, useless mixture of] vinegar on soda, is he who [thoughtlessly] sings [joyful] songs to a heavy heart."Proverbs 25:19-20 AMP

He concluded to share his pains with his superiors in the faith. He may be ridiculed by members of his congregation especially on issues that affected his matrimonial privacy. He knew that the space for privacy, integrity, sincerity and openness should not be abused. There was no doubt that he and his wife, though certified marriage counsellors, needed help in their marriage.

He consulted with Pastor Rufus who engaged him in tutorials on matrimonial sanity and serenity. He said: "Marriage is an institution where no man graduates. It is a continuous learning process. I thank God for the testimony of the relationship between you and your wife since you both came together. Her coming into your life had been of a great blessing both in your life and ministry. I am happy you both have good understanding of your temperamental differences. You must have glossed over some of the teachings I gave your youth group in those good old days. From all you have told me about her, she was just being the woman God created her to be." Donald felt he made a mistake to have brought the issues up to his trusted father in the Lord. He felt he was protective of his wife and was taking side on the issues. He, however, remembered one of the quotes of his revered mentor;"You see first in others, what you hate in yourself." He agreed in himself to listen more than attempt to exonerate or absolve himself of any error. His mentor went on: "May I ask you some questions that may open your eyes of understanding of the probable root cause of your challenges?

When last did you both pray together?

Have you agreed to continue to live in line with your knowledge of her person?

Are you already getting fed up of her quest for power and control?

Do you now feel she has no respect for your opinions?

Are you intimidated by her more possessive approach to the running of the church?

Have you ever condoned undue intimacy with any of the female members of the church?

How often do you make the mistake of making an announcement outside of her knowledge?

Do you really carry her along on decision making or do you depend solely on the board of the church?

How much attention do you give to the children as a father?

What is your financial management like?

How much do you care for her parents, siblings or extended family?

How much interest do you show in her concerns?

I hope you are not a victim of the "Is that all syndrome." Most men do not realize the "infection or virus until five years into marriage.

How much of unspoken objections do you have in your relationship?

If you feel convicted of any of these probabilities that may be the root cause of your matrimonial challenges. You need to come to the same page with your wife if you want to experience fulfillment in your ministerial calling. Your insensitivity to these facts and factors may have bad effect on the fulfillment of your calling," his mentor asserted.

With a deep sigh and drop of his head, he said: "Which way forward?"

"Are you guilty of any of these common mistakes?" he was questioned.

"Well! Not all, but a sizable number of them."

With laughter, Pastor Rufus said; "Welcome to the club. Your best bet is to right your wrongs. Remember

the statement of Jesus after his admonition to the disciples: "If you know these things, you are blessed [happy and favored by God] if you put them into practice [and faithfully do them]."
John 13:17 AMP
Your family life comes before your ministry. You may not fulfill your calling if your home is in a chaotic situation. He took his Bible and read:
"This is a faithful and trustworthy saying: if any man [eagerly] seeks the office of overseer (bishop, superintendent), he desires an excellent task. Now an overseer must be blameless and beyond reproach, the husband of one wife, self-controlled, sensible, respectable, hospitable, able to teach, not addicted to wine, not a bully nor quick-tempered and hot-headed, but gentle and considerate, free from the love of money [not greedy for wealth and its inherent power—financially ethical]. He must manage his own household well, keeping his children under control with all dignity [keeping them respectful and well-behaved] (for if a man does not know how to manage his own household, how will he take care of the church of God?)." 1 Timothy 3:1-5 AMP

The meeting of Donald with his mentor was the answer to the prayers of Ruth, his dynamic wife. She was overwhelmed by the challenges in her marriage and had engaged in intense prayer sessions for the Lord to resolve the conflicting situation between her and her husband. Though she had a disposition that suggested boldness and strength, she had no strength for stress. She wanted a smooth marital experience. The challenging situation had wounded her spirit badly. She struggled with the idea of acting contrary to her temperamental disposition but to no avail. She determined to completely yield herself to the dictate of the Holy Spirit. Her key prayer was that her husband should understand how to harness her good qualities for the betterment of their relationship. She was greatly helped by the knowledge and guidance she received when she read the book:

"PASTORS' WIFE PRAYING MANUAL"
written by Pastor Grace Okonrende

Pastor Rufus, in his final statements during his counseling with Donald, made a reference to Apostle Peter as he stated:

"In the same way, you husbands, live with your wives in an understanding way [with great gentleness and tact, and with an intelligent regard for the marriage relationship], as with someone physically weaker, since she is a woman. Show her honor and respect as a fellow heir of the grace of life, so that your prayers will not be hindered or ineffective."1 Peter 3:7 AMP
He went on: "I have no doubt that you are prayerful. Just as you have heard me read, the answer to your

prayers will be determined by the agreement between you and your wife. You could successfully go solo at the place of prayers when you were not married. However, now that you have gotten married you must make your marriage work if you want your prayers to be answered. Your agreement is of great importance for the efficacy of your prayers. Remember the affirmative statement of our Lord and Savior, Jesus Christ.

"Again I say to you, that if two believers on earth agree [that is, are of one mind, in harmony] about anything that they ask [within the will of God], it will be done for them by My Father in heaven."
Matthew 18:19 AMP

In the book of Prophet Amos Chapter 3: 3, the Bible states: "Shall two walk together, except they have agreed?"

You have to give whatever it takes to be in agreement with your wife so that your prayers will be efficacious; this is part of the secrets of church growth and success in the fulfillment of your calling.

Looking straight into the eyes of Donald, he said: "Do you have any question before we pray?" "With a little hesitation, Donald moved his head to signal: "No question" but, followed up with a statement: "Sir, I am only thinking of how to apply all that I have learnt tonight. I wish we get to talk together on the issue of marital relationship in the near future. My prayer is that it should not be an emergency meeting such as we just had. They had a short prayer session at which Pastor Rufus prayed thus: "Father, I thank you for the marriage of your daughter and your son; the level of their success, both in marriage and in the ministry. Lord, I pray that you continue to make them model and modest. You have blessed them; please do not let them have a better yesterday. Whatever be the source of contentions in their marriage, Father, intervene in the mighty name of Jesus Christ. Please grant them a perfect reconciliation in their spirit, soul and body. Let them not be a stumbling block to those who look up to them to feel your presence. Thank you for the height you have planned to take them in the ministry. Make the best of them and help them to make the best of your grace. Thank you for answered prayer, in Jesus mighty name I prayed." Donald responded with a resounding "Amen."

As they walked towards the door, Donald said: "Sir, I thank the Lord that it was to you I came. I realize that the person that gives one counsel at a challenging moment is very crucial. My coming to you and your wonderful assistance has been a divine rescue made manifest in the physical. Counseling could make or mar the circumstance or the entire life of the person being counseled. You have positively impacted my

life. Our meeting today actually reminded me of your teachings on Ministerial Comportment.
It was a successful and fulfilling moment.

CHAPTER TEN

MINISTERIAL COMPORTMENT

Donald had a burning desire for a perfect relationship between him and Ruth, his wife. He could not get over the invaluable counseling session he just had with his pastor and mentor. He respected his consistency and adherence to the teachings and dogmas of Jesus Christ. His rating of his pastor greatly improved. He strongly desired a revisit of his old notebook which contained predominantly the teachings of Pastor Rufus.

Flipping through the pages, he found the notes he took at a teaching session delivered by Pastor Rufus. It was titled: "MINISTERIAL COMPORTMENT"

He remembered his pastor's attempt to sensitize them for the teaching; especially because many of them were not ordained ministers as at the time he did the teaching. He said: "Every adult was once a baby; they only become adults because they successfully defied the agents of infant mortality. We pray the "babies" of today become reliable adults of tomorrow. A convert today has the potentials of becoming an ordained minister in the near future. A teaching on ministerial comportment may not necessarily be confined to the circles of the ordained minister of the gospel of Jesus Christ."

It was the practice of Pastor Rufus to give the definitions of the key words in any topic of his teachings. Donald soliloquized: "My pastor is a wonderful teacher." As he read:

"The meaning of a minister": A minister is:

1]. A person who accepts the responsibility of leadership of governmental organization with a mandate.

2]. A respected or coopted person who accepts the responsibility to serve others, irrespective of age, gender, race or ethnicity.

3]. A person, who on the basis of faith and commitment to a cause, accepts the responsibility to serve and meet with humility, the needs of others.

Every Christian is divinely commissioned as a prospective minister of the gospel. It is not the human ordination or organizational acknowledgement that actually makes a person a minister of the gospel of Christ."

He ruminated over the statement:

"It is not the human ordination or organizational acknowledgement that actually makes a person a minister of the gospel of Christ." It dawned on him that he was already playing the role of a pastor before

he was actually acknowledged and ordained by the authority of the church. In his soliloquy, he muttered; "Why do people struggle for titles and accolades in the church these days?" He laughed hysterically when he remembered the case of a said guest minister who refused to answer the call to the podium because he was introduced as a pastor. When the minister that sat next to him called his attention to the fact that it was time for him to go to the altar, he responded: "I am not just a pastor, I am a Bishop!" His hysteria caught the attention of his wife who had not seen him that excited in recent time. He shared his soliloquy with her and they both laughed. It was a good bonding. His imagination on the recent disaffection between him and his wife was of great concern to him. He could never have imagined there would be a moment in their relationship when there would be an "eclipse". To him, the experience was a painful "matrimonial-knockdown." He took consolation in the statement of one or two of the heavyweight boxing champions of the world:

"If you feel the pain, you are still in the game."
Evander Holyfield.

"It is no time to blame anybody; I take it as a man."
Anthony Joshua

Comportment means:

1]. The behavior or bearing of an individual.
2]. The evident idiosyncrasies of an individual. [distinctive and peculiar feature.]
3]. The mode and style of communication of an individual.

He remembered the gesticulation of his pastor in the course of the teachings; how he mimicked ladies. He said they may not utter a word but the action, reactions or inactions speak volume. It was very animating reading through his notes. It brought about old memories. He actually had fun recalling the old time. He recalled names of the brethren with whom he served and could not imagine where some of them were. He was a little disturbed when he thought of one of the brethren that was said to have backslidden before he died in an auto accident. It was on this note that his wife strolled in, as she sensed the turmoil in her husband's soul. She questioned; "What went wrong?" "I just remembered Brother Rex, as I was recalling those old good days. Ruth was emotional, and tears rolled down her cheeks. She remembered that Bro. Rex was her first desired candidate as a prospective husband. This recall added to her trauma during the very recent conflict in her marriage. She could not express the real cause of her tears. Donald, in his assumption, counted the tears as one of the usual exaggerations as typical of the choleric.

He was curious to read through the Bible passages used by his pastor during the teachings. He took his Bible, opened to 2 Corinthians. 3: 1-6.

"Are we starting to commend ourselves again? Or do we need, like some [false teachers], letters of recommendation to you or from you? [No!] You are our letter [of recommendation], written in our hearts, recognized and read by everyone. You show that you are a letter from Christ, delivered by us, written not with ink but with the Spirit of the living God, not on tablets of stone but on tablets of human hearts. Such is the confidence and steadfast reliance and absolute trust that we have through Christ toward God. Not that we are sufficiently qualified in ourselves to claim anything as coming from us, but our sufficiency and qualifications come from God. He has qualified us [making us sufficient] as ministers of a new covenant [of salvation through Christ], not of the letter [of a written code] but of the Spirit; for the letter [of the Law] kills [by revealing sin and demanding obedience], but the Spirit gives life."

He ruminated over the content of the text. In his analysis of the text, he concluded that:

1. Desire for recognition or recommendation from people can lead to frustration.
2. Many people read the life of a Christian than they have time for their Bibles.

3. The life of a Christian has a lasting impact and impression on the observers. It is a fact that no one is given a second chance to make first impression.
4. A worthy Christian should be a reliable person in whom others could have confidence.
5. Every Christian should be dependent on God. Man may always fail or disappoint and frustrate expectations.
6. A minister should of necessity have adequate cranium (head) knowledge of the scriptures; however should be led by the Holy Spirit in the interpretation and application of the word of God.

He remembered the regular statement of Pastor Rufus: "It is my determination to pass to you what my fathers in the faith committed into my hands."
His note reminded him of the source of his personal confessions and determinations:
In the depth of his thoughts, he counseled himself:
"As a Christian worker, I must be determined to be able to say as Apostle Paul wrote: 2Timothy. 3: 10, 1Corinthians. 11: 1, 23, 1 Corinthians15:3, Philippians 4: 9, Hebrews 13: 7.

"Now you have diligently followed [my example that is] my teaching, conduct, purpose, faith, patience, love, steadfastness,"2 Timothy 3:10 AMP

"Imitate me, just as I imitate Christ." 1 Cor. 11:1 AMP

"For I received from the Lord Himself that [instruction] which I passed on to you, that the Lord Jesus on the night in which He was betrayed took bread;" 1 Corinthians 11:23 AMP

"For I passed on to you as of first importance what I also received, that Christ died for our sins according to [that which] the Scriptures [foretold],"
1 Corinthians 15:3 AMP

"The things which you have learned and received and heard and seen in me, practice these things [in daily life], and the God [who is the source] of peace and well-being will be with you." Philippians 4:9 AMP.

"Remember your leaders [for it was they] who brought you the word of God; and consider the result of their conduct [the outcome of their godly lives], and imitate their faith [their conviction that God exists and is the Creator and Ruler of all things, the Provider of eternal salvation through Christ, and imitate their reliance on God with absolute trust and confidence in His power, wisdom, and goodness]." Hebrews 13:7 AMP.

I guess the conflicting situation had done more good than harm to my personal life. I would not have had any reason to visit my archives," he asserted. He turned to the next page of his notebook. He was fascinated by the sub title:

FACTORS THAT DETERMINE
PERSONAL COMPORTMENT

1]. Personality:
Do not condemn yourself for any unpleasant behavioral pattern that are related to your temperamental disposition but yield yourself to the control of the Holy Spirit. [These factors may have negative or positive effect. Please work on them in yourself].

A . Traits— temperamental or genetic.

B. Physical size. [tall, short, lanky, fat....]

C. Formative upbringing. — biological and spiritual. [Value placement...]

With a squint, he attempted a reflection on the occasion when the teaching was conducted. He could not remember all that the pastor said on the subject of personality. He wondered whether the teaching session was actually recorded on audio or video. He desired something more detailed than what he had in his notebook.

2. Environment or Setting. [Family type, position in the family, financials]

Reading about environment reminded him of his childhood days. Being the last born of the family, he knew the level of indulgence to which he was exposed. He had the understanding that indulgence is not an expression of love but a bait of destruction as defined by his pastor and mentor. In his personal analysis, environment plays a crucial role in the life of any individual. With a smile, he gleaned over his personal struggles on the impact of his childhood indulgences, pranks and rascality. He was very grateful to God for the salvation of his soul. He could not imagine where he would have been if he did not surrender his life to Jesus. There was no doubt that his youthful exuberance had been converted by the Lord to spice up his ministerial activities.

3. Association. [Class, occasions, peer...]
Donald found it difficult to let go of his notebook as every word or statement were of cogent facts and information. He remembered his childhood days and the class of people he associated with. He was very grateful to God for the appreciable progress he had made in life. His progressive success had overridden the abject poverty which was the identity of his youthful days. The statement of his pastor, "Education is a bridge, industry is the unifier," was of great relevance to him. His Master's degree in Economics had boosted his ego. He determined to do his best to conquer poverty for life. He took his Bible and read:
"A man's gift [given in love or courtesy] makes room for him and brings him before great men."
Proverbs 18:16 AMP

"Do you see a man skillful and experienced in his work? He will stand [in honor] before kings; He will not stand before obscure men."Proverbs 22:29 AMP

There was not the least doubt in his mind that he was set to be a success in life. His ministerial duties had connected him with the cream of the society within and outside of the Christian community. He was very cautious of the spirituality of his calling. His only caution was paranoia, lest he takes the spirit of suspicion for discernment."

4. Expectations. [Taste or appearance, behavioral, courtesy.]

He glared at the word, 'expectation' as if it were a new word. He had great confidence and assurance of faith that he must be a "success". He once heard Pastor Rufus say: "Many may doubt or challenge your success but may not dare a challenge when you become a "success"." He determined to put in his best in every endeavor. It was his personal belief that: "Divine endorsement is the key to commensurate reward, especially to the favored of the Lord.

He laughed at himself when he remembered his complaints at one of the hotels where he once lodged. Compared with his youthful days, that was a luxury; thanks be to the Lord that his class and expectations have changed. He dressed nicely, a match to his status as a pastor and a gifted economist on his way to bagging his PhD. He had learnt to comport himself to reflect the class to which he belonged without any iota of derision of the less privileged.

5. Relationship with the Holy Spirit. The aftermath of Grandma Eunice's death was a big blow to the entire church. It compelled Pastor Donald to develop a better relationship with the Holy Spirit. It was an evident proof of the fact that challenges will either make or mar the challenged. He was almost able to say as Apostle Paul said: "I thank God that I speak in [unknown] tongues more than all of you. 1 Corinthians 14:18 AMP.

God had been very gracious to him. His intimacy with the Holy Spirit had enhanced his relationship with his wife. Things were in near perfect condition in ministerial and domestic aspects of their lives. It suddenly dawned on him that his relationship with the Holy Spirit had greatly influenced his life and relationship with humanity. He remembered the regular statement of his pastor: "Whatever the Holy Spirit cannot resolve, man cannot undo." He reached for his Bible and read: "I have told you these things while I am still with you. But the Helper (Comforter, Advocate, Intercessor—Counselor, Strengthener, Standby), the Holy Spirit, whom the Father will send in My name [in My place, to represent Me and act on My behalf], He will teach you all things. And He will help you remember everything that I have told you." John 14:25-26 AMP

Consequences and reward

It was not difficult for him to remember almost all the explanations of his pastor on consequences and rewards. He was said to have explained: "These are basic factors that motivate or restrain humanity. It is very important for man to understand the implications of actions, reactions or inaction, when and what is morally expedient. He quoted some scriptures he had committed to memory: "Everything is permissible for me, but not all things are beneficial. Everything is permissible for me, but I will not be enslaved by anything [and brought under its power, allowing it to control me]." 1 Corinthians 6:12 AMP.

"All things are lawful [that is, morally legitimate, permissible], but not all things are beneficial or advantageous. All things are lawful, but not all things are constructive [to character] and edifying [to spiritual life]. 1 Corinthians 10:23 AMP.

"Only be careful that this liberty of yours [this power to choose] does not somehow become a stumbling block [that is, a temptation to sin] to the weak [in conscience]. 1 Corinthians 8:9 AMP. "But whoever causes one of these little ones who believe in Me to stumble and sin [by leading him away from My teaching], it would be better for him to have a heavy millstone [as large as one turned by a donkey] hung around his neck and to be drowned in the depth of the sea." Matthew 18:6 AMP. "And angels who did not keep their own designated place of power, but abandoned their proper dwelling place, [these] He has kept in eternal chains under [the thick gloom of utter] darkness for the judgment of the great day,". Jude 1:6 AMP.

He could almost hear in retrospect the closing statement of his pastor: "You cannot afford to slaughter your ultimate on the altar of your immediate. As important as these factors are, they should not be the only determinants of the comportment of a minister of the gospel. A minister of the gospel is expected to be guided and led by the Holy Spirit. The led however must be sure that the leading is in conformity with the standard word of God."

RELATIONSHIP WITH OTHERS
[Ministers and Members]

Going through his note book was a unique reconnection with memory lane. He could almost audibly hear his pastor say:

#. "The position of a minister of the gospel calls for self-discipline and respect with zero tolerance for self-indulgence."

#. "Respect must be earned not demanded."

#. "Respect is accorded based on the integrity of the would be respected."

#. "The conformity with expedience earns more respect than legality."
#. "Relevance and significance are determined by the ability to meet the needs of others."
#. "Be tolerant, remember: "The good are the pained." When others call you "GOOD" they must have gotten away with some offenses, taken advantage, insults and assaults that compel their respect for your person."
#. "Understand that everyone is entitled to his or her own opinion."
#. "Learn to respect the opinions of others even when they are at variance with yours."
#. "When your opinion is at variance with that of others, look more inward than projecting your objections."
#. "When objection to the opinion of others becomes mandatory, be very firm and friendly. Start your objection with the phrase: "With all due respect. Sir/Ma."
#. "Do not insist on having the last say."
#. "Prefer to suffer wrong instead of unnecessary contention or altercation. "
#. As much as possible, avoid discussion of politics on your platform or in the midst of your members or ministers. Politics may divide or polarize your church.
#. "When on telephone conversation, learn to listen than speak. Do not hang up the phone until you have

said: "good-bye" and you heard the same from the other side of the line."

#. Maintain neutrality in the resolve of matrimonial issues between couples or siblings.

#. "When talking with your superior, let him or her hang up the phone first."

#. "Be very respectful in your use of language and gestures. Words like, Sir, Ma, Please, Pardon... are "miracle words.""

#. "Be a blessing to your pastors and ministers. Support their travels and supply what you think they may have need of."

#. "Do not visit or remain in a secluded place with opposite sex, especially of the same age-range, at odd times of the day without the presence or company of others."

#. "It is very important that you notify your pastor or immediate superior officer before you embark on a journey."

#. "As a superior officer; please notify your immediate junior officer about your movements especially when you are traveling out of state."

#. "As a superior officer, do not correct your erring officer in the open, especially in the presence of his or her subordinate. Only call a recalcitrant officer to order when the said officer had breached or flaunted instructions with impunity."

#. "If you have members of your extended family in your local assembly or your areas of jurisdiction, make sure you do not create room for nepotism or any suspicion of favoritism."

#. "It is very important that you do not share with your spouse official confidential issues, especially if he or she is not involved with the policy making body."

#. "As much as possible, only exercise the spirit of discernment, not the spirit of suspicion. Let people around you be at liberty, especially your spouse."

#. "Have a good respect for the elders and the elderly."

#. "Treasure old age, not muddled brain."

#. "Do not make promises you are not ready to fulfill; all things being equal."

#. "Understand that most parents protect the interest of their children. Make the children your priority if you intend to retain the membership of their parents."

#. "Make the best of your time. Value your effectiveness to the collective than any individual's domination of you or your time."

#. Plan ahead of time for effective implementation and success of your program.

#. "Give priority to your family, except the Lord demands otherwise."

#. "Maintain your integrity by the application of uniform standard on the way issues are handled."

#. "Always remember that example is better than precept. Be model and modest as a leader or minister."

#. "Realize that trust and confidence are born out of faithfulness and honesty.

#. When you invite a guest speaker, treat him or her with utmost respect. It is expedient that you make adequate arrangement for the prompt pickup of your guest."

#. "Do your best to be sure that you or your protocol officers are at the airport before the arrival of your guest speaker. Don't ever leave your guest waiting or stranded."

#. "Make sure the hotel room is fully ready before the arrival of your guest. Do not take your guest to the reception to collect the key to the hotel room."

#. "If possible, do not keep your guest speaker in your home except a guest with whom you have a very strong family bond. Remember; familiarity breeds contempt."

#. "Always remember that travel is a risk; treat your guest right."

#. "When you are redeployed, do not probe into the activities of your successor or maintain undue attachment with your previous team or congregation. They belong to God."

#. "Don't undermine your successor. It disrupts sanity and integrity in the system."

#. "Do not undermine the authority of your leaders, directly or indirectly before your subordinates. Always remember that they are entitled to their opinions on issues. If you do, you must have shot yourself in the leg. They may inevitably undermine you."

#. "Do not be sarcastic when passing the instructions of your leader to your colleagues or subordinates."

#. If you become very successful in the ministry, always remember your good friends of old, they are in most cases more reliable than the new ones

#. Always understand that you are the "Bible" most of the people read.

"You are our letter [of recommendation], written in our hearts, recognized and read by everyone. You show that you are a letter from Christ, delivered by us, written not with ink but with the Spirit of the living God, not on tablets of stone but on tablets of human hearts." 2 Corinthians 3:2-3 AMP

Honoring an invitation

The subheading: **"Honoring an invitation"** triggered his laughter when he remembered the story of a guest speaker who refused to eat what was served by his host but requested for an oriental cereal which was almost impossible for the hospitality team to find in the market. He eventually delayed the protocol, thus he got late to the meeting.

He read his notes, taken during the teachings by Pastor Rufus:

#. "When you are offered a hand of fellowship for ministration, do your best to show appreciation and respect for your host.

#. Appreciate the spouse of your host if he or she is married.

#. Appreciate the team of ministers of the ministry; do not forget to commend the workers.

#. Let your acceptance of invitation be based on conviction.

#. Listen to the Holy Spirit, not the financial viability of the congregation that invited you. Be there to honor the Lord.

#. Remember, ministry is a call to service and sacrifice.

#. Let your host determine the level of comfort they can afford without unnecessary strain.

#. Do not dictate the standard. Should the standard be below your expectation, upgrade yourself. Notify your host about your intention before the upgrade. If you cannot afford the upgrade, that obviously speaks volume.

#. Ask for the guiding rules of the local system. Understand that your compliance will add credence to your integrity.

#. Do not overshoot the stipulated or allotted time. Realize that it is an insult on your host to ask the congregation whether you should continue preaching when your allotted time had expired. 1Cor. 14: 32-33

#. Never display any air or impression of superiority. If superiority is acknowledged by your host, please display humility.

#. Do not attempt to force your way through, if your host cannot meet your expectations.

#. If you are displeased with the quality of the dishes served, register your displeasure with utmost humility.

#. Treat your servers [The hospitality team] with respect.

#. Channel all your requests through your host or designated officers.

#. Do not circumvent your host to discuss your desires or needs with members of the church, even if you have met with them long before being invited.

#. Always realize that you are a minister of the gospel of Christ not of money.

Avoid being blinded by money.

#. Realize that honorarium has been a contentious issue amongst religious sects these days. Avoid being dragged into the negotiation game.

#. Appreciate every gift and the givers. It is not the value but the love that counts.

#. Go to places you are led by the Spirit. If your experience was bad or your spirit does not flow or approve of a particular invitation or place, please decline the invitation or subsequent invitations with humility.

#. Go to places where the Spirit of Christ and the grace of God upon your life are celebrated not merely tolerated.

#. Spend a good time at the place of prayers.

#. Always remember that whatever the Holy Spirit cannot resolve, man cannot undo."

Jesus said:
"I will not speak with you much longer, for the ruler of the world (Satan) is coming. And he has no claim on Me [no power over Me nor anything that he can use against Me]; but so that the world may know [without any doubt] that I love the Father, I do exactly as the Father has commanded Me [and act in full agreement with Him]. Get up, let us go from here."
John 14:30-31 AMP.

"I assure you and most solemnly say to you, a slave is not greater than his master, nor is one who is sent greater than the one who sent him. If you know these things, you are blessed [happy and favored by God] if you put them into practice [and faithfully do them]."
John 13:16-17 AMP

It is very important that a minister of the gospel of Christ walk worthy of the calling.

Apostle Paul wrote:
"So I, the prisoner for the Lord, appeal to you to live a life worthy of the calling to which you have been called [that is, to live a life that exhibits godly character, moral courage, personal integrity, and mature behavior—a life that expresses gratitude to God for your salvation], with all humility [forsaking self-righteousness], and gentleness [maintaining self-control], with patience, bearing with one another in

[unselfish] love. Make every effort to keep the oneness of the Spirit in the bond of peace [each individual working together to make the whole successful]."
Ephesians 4:1-3 AMP

"I assure you and most solemnly say to you, a slave is not greater than his master, nor is one who is sent greater than the one who sent him. If you know these things, you are blessed [happy and favored by God] if you put them into practice [and faithfully do them]."
John 13:16-17 AMP

Donald was very appreciative of the counseling session he had with Pastor Rufus. The teachings were of tremendous blessings to him. In his personal resolve and conclusions, he read:

"Watch over your heart with all diligence, for from it flows the springs of life. Put away from you a deceitful (lying, misleading) mouth, and put devious lips far from you. Let your eyes look directly ahead [toward the path of moral courage] And let your gaze be fixed straight in front of you [toward the path of integrity]. Consider well and watch carefully the path of your feet, And all your ways will be steadfast and sure. Do not turn away to the right nor to the left [where evil may lurk]; Turn your foot from [the path of] evil."
Proverbs 4:23-27 AMP

He remembered his mentor once told him:

"You may not live better or excel beyond your thought life."

He conclusively read from Apostle Paul's letter to the Philippians:

"Finally, believers, whatever is true, whatever is honorable and worthy of respect, whatever is right and confirmed by God's word, whatever is pure and wholesome, whatever is lovely and brings peace, whatever is admirable and of good repute; if there is any excellence, if there is anything worthy of praise, think continually on these things [center your mind on them, and implant them in your heart]. The things which you have learned and received and heard and seen in me, practice these things [in daily life], and the God [who is the source] of peace and well-being will be with you."

Philippians 4:8-9 AMP

He had a fair understanding of the spirituality of his calling as he read a text from John the beloved:

"Beloved, we are [even here and] now children of God, and it is not yet made clear what we will be [after His coming]. We know that when He comes and is revealed, we will [as His children] be like Him, because we will see Him just as He is [in all His glory]. And everyone who has this hope [confidently placed] in Him purifies himself, just as He is pure (holy, undefiled, guiltless)." 1 John 3:2-3 AMP

Decision Page

I want to invite you to make Jesus your Lord and personal savior if you have not done so. Boycott Hell and embrace eternal life given through believing in Jesus as your Lord and personal savior. Prayer and fasting will not work if you do not belong to the kingdom of God, and if you don't with sincerity of heart declare for Jesus. If today, you agree to give your life to Jesus, the sample prayer below will change your life and relationship for the better. God is the author of marriage; He will give you the best of it.

Please pray:
Dear Jesus, I believe you died for me and that you rose again on the third day. I confess to you that I am a sinner and that I need your love and forgiveness. Come into my life, forgive my sins, and turn my life around. With my mouth I confess that you are the son of God. In my heart I believe that God raised you from the dead. I declare that you are my Lord and Master. Thank You Jesus. From today, help me to walk in your peace, love, forgiveness and joy forever.
Signed: _____

Date: _____

Call for counseling or ministration
Contact me at: 832-723-8470

About the Author

Pastor Ade Okonrende is the product of the union between Samuel Akinlabi and Henrietta Ojuolape Okonrende nee Adeseolu. They both hailed from Abeokuta, Ogun State, Nigeria.

Samuel Okonrende became a polygamist with four wives. It was his plan just to train the first male child of each of the wives. This gave Ade little or no chance to higher education because he was the second surviving male child of his mother. His mother very much valued education. It was her determination that afforded all her children the attainment of appreciable academic qualifications.

Ade Okonrende is an alumnus of the UNIVERSITY OF IFE now OBAFEMI AWOLOWO UNIVERSITY, Ile-Ife, Nigeria and THE REDEEMED CHRISTIAN BIBLE COLLEGE, London. He pioneered The RCCG in London; 1990-1999 before he relocated to USA with his family in 1999. His family ministry was officially launched in London in 1995 in commemoration of ten years of marriage

Along with his wife they have published many books and over one hundred thousand pamphlets (Family Issues) on Christian Marriage.

He is a Regional Pastor in the RCCGNA. He is directly in-charge of peace and reconciliation. He currently serves as the Senior Pastor of RCCGNA Pavilion of Redemption, 15227 Old Richmond Road, Sugarland, Texas USA.

His marriage is blessed with four children: Grace, Chosen, Choice and Royal and increasing grand children to the glory of God.

Notes

_____

_____

_____

_____

_____

_____

_____

_____

_____

_____

_____

_____

_____

_____

_____

_____

_____

Other books by author
ORDER YOUR COPIES NOW!

Available at: Amazon.com
choiceworldpublishers.com
832-723-8470; 832-372-0860

Available at: Amazon.com
choiceworldpublishers.com
832-723-8470; 832-372-0860